SILENT SAFETY

BEST PRACTICES FOR
PROTECTING THE AFFLUENT

Library of Congress Control Number: 2010921194
ISBN-13: 978-0-9800398-3-2
ISBN-10: 0-9800398-3-5

Worth
From the publisher of Worth magazine
www.worth.com

Sandow Media
Corporate Headquarters
3731 NW 8th Avenue
Boca Raton, FL 33431
www.sandowmedia.com

For information regarding sales and bulk purchases, please contact
silentsafety@sandowmedia.com

Printed in the United States of America
First edition: February 2010
10 9 8 7 6 5 4 3 2 1

DEDICATIONS

Dedicated to the memory of
Michael Viollis and Robert "Bob" Kane

It is with commitment and compassion to all Alzheimer's victims
that we joined this fight by forming the RCS Alzheimer's Foundation,
providing researchers with ongoing financial support. We stand
committed to battling this disease through our fundraising
efforts and proceeds received from this book.

Thank you for your contribution.
rcsalzfoundation.org

TABLE OF CONTENTS

FOREWORD

I would rather not live in the world of Paul Viollis and Doug Kane. All too often, it is a scary place in which terrible things can happen to good people because of criminals who want what they have. Children are kidnapped. Human beings who've made the mistake of being human get blackmailed. Successful people worry that their homes will be broken into, their identities will be stolen or someone will abscond with the fruits of their labor.

No. When all is said and done, I'd prefer to live in a world where everyone gets along; we can all leave our doors unlocked; the babysitter is always trustworthy; and we live to a ripe, happy and healthy old age in a town where everyone wishes each other goodnight like the Waltons.

But I don't expect that's going to happen any time soon. The truth is, I do live in Paul and Doug's world, and whether you like it or not, whether you acknowledge it or not, so do you. Regardless of our station in life, we all face threats. We just don't want to admit how dangerous the planet can be. It's stressful to think of how constantly we are surrounded by bad intentions. Most of us, if we had to think about the subject every day, 24/7, wouldn't hold up under the pressure.

We want to feel safe; we want to be safe. But we don't want to spend the time, energy and mental rigor necessary to ensure our safety. Because we don't want our lives to be filled with so much danger, even when they are. That's a burden most of us don't want.

I thought about this paradox when I recently visited Paul and Doug in the Manhattan offices of their firm, Risk Control Strategies, and spoke with them and their crack team of security experts. Surrounded by flashing computer monitors and alarms hooked up to faraway places, these guys think about bad stuff and bad guys 24/7, and they do it so that, at least most of the time, the people they work for don't have to. I listened as Paul and Doug talked about the world beyond my everyday borders, and I realized that— while most of us live our days going about our business, going to our jobs, raising our families, taking in a

Yankees game or popping in a Netflix—some people, a lot more than I had really ever thought about, spend their days pondering how to commit crimes. And because of how technology is changing the world, those crimes were often things I didn't even know existed.

But I also heard Paul and Doug talk about how they and their team work to anticipate and prevent those crimes or, when necessary, solve them. And that was reassuring. Because I realized that, while I may not think about the dangers around us very much, Paul Viollis and Doug Kane do, and they do it so that people like you and me can sleep at night. And I knew that, if I have to live in Paul and Doug's world, I'm awfully glad that they're in it.

Richard Bradley
Editor-in-chief, *Worth Magazine*
October 2009

WHY READ SILENT SAFETY?

As the nation's financial crisis continues to make headlines, many affluent families' clear and present dangers may be flying under the radar. Wealth brings considerable attention and security exposure to families across the globe. Many take appropriate countermeasures only after costly, disruptive or embarrassing events unfold. Since the inception of Risk Control Strategies (RCS), we have provided security solutions for the high-net-worth community to include some of the most affluent families in North America. At the behest of many and driven by copious experiences, it was our desire to craft a true, personal security best-practice reference book for the affluent and their advisors. The information to follow will crystallize the various risks families face everyday. We will provide pragmatic advice and strategic countermeasures that can be immediately deployed to contain a crisis, as well as recommendations to preemptively mitigate risk. These pages will provide you with our proven methodology for protecting the wealthy and providing them with peace of mind.

Security is not merely a function of investing large amounts of money in countermeasures that may or may not address the types of threats facing a particular family. Oftentimes, small changes can be implemented that dramatically reduce exposure. It is the result of very specific methodologies we have developed and continually deploy, taking a long-term view of security that can be easily modified as personal needs or external factors change. After risks have been identified and we have obtained an understanding of the families' activities, we develop a comprehensive approach to security and safety, providing our clients the ultimate gift of confidence and well-being.

We have witnessed firsthand that the majority of individuals who are considered the ultra affluent spend an insufficient amount of time thinking about security unless they have already been victimized. They live in gated communities that are easily accessed and have alarm systems that are inadequate and rarely armed. They believe that, because they live in prestigious neighborhoods and there is a security patrol nearby, they can turn a blind eye to security for themselves and their families. The general belief is that "this only happens to other people who live in other places." To understand why that statement is false, you merely have to watch or listen to the numerous news outlets (without immediately changing the channel) reporting the compounding risks we face, which are increasing annually. No one is immune to becoming a victim, and the risks are dramatically exacerbated for the wealthy individual. This requires that proactive steps be taken to safeguard one's most important assets.

During our collective careers, we have arrested hundreds of criminals from all walks of life. They include kidnappers, murderers, serial killers, bank robbers, rapists, child molesters, thieves of all kinds, fugitives, terrorists, drug dealers and white-collar criminals. Many of these individuals blended into their respective communities and preyed upon the weak and innocent at every opportunity. The one common denominator we have learned was that, for the most part, they committed their respective crimes only when they thought they could get away. They made decisions based upon the security observed and the alertness of their intended victims. Just as we would thoroughly investigate a subject's background and learn about their activities prior to confronting him or her, these individuals employ the same tactics upon their intended prey.

The good news is that you can implement effective and proven security procedures to minimize the inherent risks presented by the 21st century intruder. That said, consider this book as an overview of the procedures that will provide you an immediate frame of reference to diagnose a situation and apply the appropriate solution. This book is not intended to provide comprehensive solutions for all security issues facing the affluent whereby the reader can independently address these issues as they surface. It is intended to be more of a guide that identifies the issues and brings them to the forefront so professionals can address them. Knowledge is power, and the more we can understand about security issues faced by the affluent, the more prepared we can become.

The RCS case files are factual; however, we are all about confidentiality, so no client names are provided, and some of the information was altered slightly to further protect client identities. Though the stories and situations primarily address the affluent community and their advisors, many areas of this book will benefit the reader regardless of net worth, as it pertains to personal security and safety.

We hope you enjoy reading this as much as we did recalling our experiences.

PROLOGUE

For more than three decades, we have dedicated our lives to the safety and well-being of the American people. As our respective careers matured, our destiny steered us into responding to a plethora of matters within the affluent community. From A-list entertainers and marquee athletes to financial industry executives and entrepreneurs, the frequency of cases ranging from kidnap and extortion to home invasion and fraud increased exponentially. We say this because it is imperative for you, the reader, to understand that what lies before you is the compilation of thousands of cases that were brought to resolution as a result of the strategies articulated herein. Hence, at the behest of numerous colleagues and clients, the genesis of this literary piece on "best practices" in protecting the affluent took shape and developed into what awaits you.

One must seize the fact that to efficiently and effectively serve the affluent community, each and every advisor must embrace their respective responsibility. Advisors must continually educate themselves in the various best practice methodologies that exist in protecting their clients' human, physical and financial assets. To adopt a laissez-faire approach to this is both irresponsible and unprofessional. To those who disagree, I pose this question: What is your margin for error when your client, who trusts you with his or her well-being, comes to you with a security-related crisis scenario? If you are unsure, consult your client and, if you haven't grasped this already, we are not crafting this to win a beauty contest but, more so, to save lives: Servare Vitas.

All operators on the F.B.I. Hostage Rescue Team (HRT) live by this motto, Servare Vitas. While team leader on HRT and subsequently the FBI SWAT team commander in Los Angeles, I was involved in numerous situations where we did just that: rescue victims, return kidnapped children to their parents and, most importantly, save lives. It was only fitting that we would adopt this same motto for RCS. We are dedicated to not only saving lives in the traditional sense, but also preserving legacies, reputations and the financial well-being of those we serve.

Our mantra is simple: to make certain that all those who read this book acquire a firm understanding of the personal security best practices required for the affluent community. That's it. Should you be considered a subject matter expert upon conclusion? I would think not. However, you should obtain the necessary information to advise and guide affluent families through the turbulent waters they may in fact encounter. With subjects ranging from threat management, investigative due diligence and securing the home front to kidnap, extortion, cyber crime, protecting children and travel security, this book will provide detailed information that will assist the risk advisor in more holistically serving clients. The content contained herein will also provide the affluent family a valid yardstick in measuring the level of service delivery they require based upon what they are receiving.

Drawing upon decades of hands-on experience, we have crafted this book to ensure the issues that cause unease are addressed and solutions illustrated within a frame the reader can digest in one sitting. Invest your time wisely, absorb this material and walk away more prepared than ever before to be the advisor others only claim to be or the matriarch/patriarch you need to be.

The Personal Security Mantra

Contrary to popular belief, the best security for an affluent family is typically that which you don't see. Apart from those few circumstances where individuals/families want a "show of force," security should be approached through preparedness measures that bring peace of mind, not overt solutions that create superfluous attention. True, this is what is typically portrayed on the big screen, but, in real life, it is not the desired path. To illustrate this point, we offer the following examples:

1. Residential Security Architecture:
Affluent families should be advised to select a preemptively designed/panel integrated solution that can neither be detected nor disarmed. This will alert them to the presence of an intruder when he first steps foot on their property instead of once he has gained access to their home. The deliverable should also include

an aesthetically pleasing CCTV solution that is strategically positioned around their estate in lieu of an easily detectable and obtrusive technology that is more susceptible to compromise and detracts from the beauty (not to mention the potential value) of their estate. Much more later . . .

2. Personal Protection:

When confronted with this request, the advisor must remember "bigger is not necessarily better." Hence, drawing more attention to your client by not properly pairing the personal protection professional (PPP) to the principal (person being protected) can substantially increase the risk. Let's cite an example by offering a test question. If the principal were a petite, 5-foot-3-inch African-American female, would you prefer a well-built, 6-foot-6-inch Caucasian man or a 5-foot-7-inch African-American female? Be honest—then justify your answer.

These two examples merely set the stage for numerous discussions to follow with the underscored message being; effective protection strategies must be congruent with the specific probability of risk and should be made known to very few.

Cheap Is Expensive

From The RCS Files – No Time to Be Frugal
RCS was retained to conduct a due diligence investigation on the principals of a large-scale development project who were allegedly putting up millions of dollars and seeking additional private financing. Though no criminal history or prior fraudulent dealings were identified, the investigation showed these individuals had few assets and did not appear to have the ability to actually produce the funding which they stated they could access. Since there were several red flags of concern, RCS recommended to the client that additional investigative work be conducted to verify the funds and their source to ensure no illegal wrongdoing was involved. The client declined and, three weeks later, called for assistance after being charged with money laundering by the F.B.I.

Cutting corners when the outcome could have a devastating impact on your life is not just ill-advised but beyond reasonable comprehension. One may argue after looking at our resumes that we share somewhat of a tainted view of the world, but then wouldn't you after spending a lifetime immersed in scenarios most people avoid thinking about so that others can sleep at night? Hold a victim until they stop shaking, convince someone so distraught that suicide is not the solution or look into parents' eyes after their child has been abducted or abused—and then tell us you can put a price tag on peace of mind. Advisors should adopt a philosophy with their clients not to roll the dice when the outcome could lead to grave consequences, and affluent individuals should not be willing to bet bad things won't happen to them.

Price is a critical element in all decisions but, unfortunately, it consistently supersedes personal security concerns. As an example, it is unfortunate but true that it is not uncommon for a family to build a multimillion dollar home and leave security as an afterthought. Once brought to their attention, they solicit suggestions from the general contractor, who recommends the same system for all his clients since he is not in the security business. There is no thought of conducting a threat assessment, evaluating the surrounding neighborhoods and understanding the family's lifestyle. Therefore, it is prudent to advise clients to understand their true risk level and to compare "apples to apples" when trying to decide upon a security-related solution and avoid looking for what's cheapest. Remember, if it is priced low, there is a reason.

Servare Vitas

The Latin phrase "Servare Vitas," meaning "to save lives," is the true benchmark of security consulting. Each advisor must embrace the responsibility of directing their clients down the path that is in their best interest, and not just go along with wishes that can cause harm. For example, what if your client asks for your opinion about opening a business in a location where kidnappings are rampant? If you support such a decision, without offering better alternatives or describing the inherent risks of his or her intentions, you will not be doing anyone any favors, including yourself. Insurance coverage for kidnap and ransom is valuable but won't change the fact they were kidnapped and victimized. Moreover, Servare Vitas extends far beyond life and death circumstances. It speaks to creating the framework for peace of mind by placing an invisible hedge around the individual/family, thus protecting all their human, financial and physical assets without hindrance to lifestyle; hence, to safeguard one's legacy.

The 21st Century Intruder

Perhaps one of the most important facts for the affluent community to remember, as well as advisors, is that this population does not attract the low- to moderate-level criminal. In fact, the sophisticated criminal is your adversary, including cyber hackers, identity thieves, con artists and those who perpetrate home invasions/burglaries.

Better prepared and equipped than ever before, the 21st century intruder conducts thorough due diligence as well as surveillance and phishing exercises before perpetrating a crime. From various international organized crime groups to very sophisticated U.S.-based criminal alliances, the affluent client (including their family office) is center stage in the threat arena. Why? Well, it's simple. This community offers the greatest return on investment for the experienced criminal. They enjoy the maximum probability of financial reward while facing minimal risk. This is based upon the fact that the affluent community typically does not thoroughly protect themselves and navigates through life with a false sense of security. Please, keep in mind as you read on that it's not personal but just business to the world's top criminals as you are targeted to be their next victim.

State of the Union

Where are the risks coming from?
Who is truly being targeted?
What should advisors be saying to keep their clients safe?
What security measures should the affluent deploy?

Primarily, the risks to the affluent community are coming from cyber trollers and hackers on the outside and those in the inner circle such as employees, contractors and advisors on the inside. The cyber criminal, many of which have yet to conclude their teenage years, begins his/her research on the Internet, seeking out wealthy individuals. They ascertain as much as they can about them online and then test the waters to see how deep they can get into their lives. Acquired personal information is used, sold or brokered to others for future deployment. So if you're wondering who is hacking into your computers and alarm systems, look no further. On the other hand, fraud, kidnap for ransom, home invasions, residential burglaries, grand theft, identity/data theft and extortion are a sampling of the crimes committed against the affluent community by their own employees and contractors. Let us not forget the Madoff-esque threat from financial advisors with nothing more than a country club resume and who become insulted when you request to verify their backgrounds. **Go figure**. Therefore, the more affluent the person, the more profitable the target or "mark" for this intruder, dispelling the common thought, "I'm not a celebrity, so I'm OK," or "No one really knows anything about me because I'm a low-key person."

In sum, the main contributing factors for these exploits are a lack of thorough background investigations, blind trust and absence of internal controls. Please bear in mind that the aforementioned points are facts. Alarming? Yes. True? Most definitely. Fixable? Without question.

Before moving forward, let's look briefly at the most prevalent risk probability factors to the affluent community:

- Wealth - The more information the world has regarding your wealth or the greater the wealth, the larger the potential threat.

- Family office - A true one-stop shop for the 21st century intruder. If this office is not protecting your information properly, don't be surprised when something happens.

- Celebrity status - Your location and tastes will forever be public knowledge. This intruder is not necessarily attracted to your money but to you.

• Neighborhood - Don't fool yourself—every affluent neighborhood in the country is nothing more than a playground for the dili-
gent intruder to break into your life.

Oh, and to address that gated community thought process—believing
people can't get in—we have but one question: How many contractors
and delivery people are permitted access to your community every day
whom you know nothing about and require no form of identification
from other than a name on a truck?

Understanding the Culture

Privacy – Confidentiality – Loyalty

Time-measured trust is the key ingredient in formulating a successful
relationship with the affluent client. Without question, the most productive way to begin any relationship is to provide the client with a
nondisclosure agreement illustrating the advisor's commitment to
protecting all information to which they are exposed.

Oftentimes, we receive calls from clients or their advisors stating exactly what they believe they need. Regardless if it is an alarm system,
protection detail, security guard or a restraining order, they want it
and want it now! Our usual response would be, "If you know exactly
what you need, then you don't need us." However, we would caution
them by giving several analogies. For instance, if you feel as though
you are having chest pains, do you tell your cardiologist you have a
blockage and you need surgery immediately? Or does the doctor
schedule an appointment so tests can be conducted to reach a diagno-
sis? If you hear a good stock tip at a cocktail party and contact your
trusted broker to invest a large amount of money, does he do so without conducting the necessary research on the company? You say, "Of
course not," since you trust their opinions—or you wouldn't be dealing
with them in the first place. Why do people look at their security
so differently?

Being that affluent clients prefer to surround themselves with individuals they trust and who understand their needs, embracing their values and beliefs is critical, which is why no two clients are exactly alike. Hence, any strategy, whether it is insurance, financial, legal or security-related, requires a diagnostic process prior to implementing the client-specific plan. To the affluent client: If you are receiving a cookie-cutter approach, don't walk—run away.

Protecting Privacy

We have determined that some of the most damaging information obtained by adversaries has been obtained inadvertently from friends and employees who are within the family's inner circle. Everyone must be cautious about giving out information on the phone regarding family members, travel plans or activities. Pretext calls are frequently used to illicit confidential and personal information. They may be initiated by former employees, acquaintances, friends or individuals purporting to be job applicants.

The following precautions should be taken on a regular basis:

• Take note of all suspicious persons loitering in the vicinity of the family, including around the residence and in public locations. Be sure to write down a complete description of the person and/or vehicle

• All trash identifying the client, family or containing confidential information should be put through a confetti-cut shredder prior to being put in the trash

• Any lost identification or confidential information needs to be immediately addressed

• Family information should be discussed on a need-to-know basis, and discussions should not take place in public locations

• Employees should immediately report any arrests or civil

litigation since this may make them a target for compromise

• Ensure all new hires are subject to thorough background investigations

• Employees who are being terminated or resign should be required to have an exit interview and be instructed that the confidentiality agreement they originally signed will remain in force

Now that we have crafted the necessary overview, the sections to follow will take you through the entire best-practice process, from diagnosing risk to the formulation and implementation of the required deliverables.

From The RCS Files – Vail Vacation
Prior to meeting with a new family, we routinely conduct a preliminary cyber search to obtain a better understanding of the family, including number of children, ages, where they attended school, hobbies, etc. It was determined that there was extensive publicly available information regarding this particular family; however, the information overall was not increasing the threat level to family members, and no pictures of the children were discovered. Further research determined a Facebook account for one of the younger daughters. Listed on the site were pictures of family members, pictures and names of the family dogs (the fact they were extremely friendly) and pictures of the family vacation home in Vail, Colorado. It was further explained when they would be there on vacation as well as other information any kidnapper, pedophile or household burglar would love to have. Do you know what your kids post on the Web?

Chapter

1

THE SECURITY DIAGNOSTIC

Crafting a Valid Threat Level

It is virtually impossible to provide a valid and reliable security solution to an affluent client without first examining the client's specific lifestyle and identifying the corresponding risks it presents. As previously stated, one must understand that there is no "cookie cutter" approach to providing security for the affluent client. That said, the following lifestyle categories must be examined carefully and specific descriptive responses to each component derived prior to formulating a plan:

- Travel patterns – mode, method, frequency, purpose and locations (domestic or international)
- Residences – locations, security measures in place, event frequency, degree of valuables on site

- Yacht/aircraft ownership – crew validation, locations maintained, frequency/purpose of use, charter/lease agreements

- Philanthropic activity – events sponsored, how well publicized, frequency of contributions, public information available

- Business interests – type, industry, public or private, media coverage

- Religious activities – public information, level of involvement, previous concerns, collateral issues

- Political involvement – active campaigner, monetary support, frequency

- Personal habits – travel, collector, hobbies, events frequently attended, predictability of actions, tastes

- Social involvement – social functions, frequency, events hosted, media coverage

- Internet usage – family members, home office, financial trading, Web surfing, gaming participation, banking

- Family office involvement – SFO/MFO internal controls, structure, personal participation, check signers

- Investment strategy – financial advisors, documented procedures and expectations, communication requirements

- Employee/contractor/advisor due diligence

Analytical Review and Implementation

Building upon information obtained in the initial examination, you are now able to begin the initial steps of designing and implementing a personal family security plan. The following preparation and services should be incorporated into the plan:

- Background investigation and vendor/contractor screening program

- Due diligence investigations on current and future business associations/partnerships

- Investment intelligence (knowing with whom you are doing business)

- Security system planning and design

- Travel security and foreign travel advisory service

- Executive protection, both domestic and international

- Special events planning

- Identity theft protection, mitigation and response

- Crisis preparation and response

- Threat management

Education and Response

This is the maintenance phase where ongoing reviews and assessments will be provided to address changing needs. Informal training seminars should be arranged to educate clients and their families in the following areas:

- Staff training

- Kidnap prevention and education

- Surviving a hostage situation

- Identifying and responding to stalking situations

- Travel security precautions

- Campus security issues

- Violence avoidance

- Personal security considerations

Yacht and Aircraft Security Measures

Security for the affluent family that owns and utilizes a private aircraft and/or yacht should evaluate and implement various security measures into an overall written plan. You should not rely on the captain and crew to be looking out for your best interests from a security perspective. You need to ensure a vulnerability assessment is conducted on the vessel, evaluating many of the areas previously discussed and also those areas which are unique to the mode of travel.

From The RCS Files - Monaco Yacht Diversion
While concluding a comprehensive security assessment for a client, we still needed to inspect their yacht and interview the crew. The vessel remained in Monaco Harbor off the coast of France for the majority of the year. It was the family's wishes to have the assessment completed on location in Monaco instead of waiting until the yacht returned to the U.S. later in the year.

The necessary information was obtained, and an RCS employee was dispatched to the Monaco location. Upon arrival, the yacht was not at its assigned docking location. Further inquiry determined the yacht had only been back to port once during the previous four weeks to take on additional provisions. The client immediately contacted the yacht's captain, on the ship's GPS telephone, and was told he was at the dock in Monaco doing routine maintenance.

The authorities were contacted, and the yacht was located in the

Mediterranean full of undocumented aliens and contraband. It was determined that, since the yacht was used so infrequently by the owners, the captain had developed a lucrative smuggling operation while still being available to the client by phone.

Yacht Security

• Identify and confirm the background of crew

• Ensure confidentiality and NDAs are in place

• Conduct periodic TSCM (sweeps) on yacht to ensure privacy

• If weapons are on board, ensure appropriate training and storage

• Determine if vessel comes under new MTSA and IMO regulations (requirements for vessel security officer); if yes, ensure training requirements are met

• Obtain continual and advanced travel itinerary for client and determine risk for each intended location via a written threat assessment (travel to foreign ports should utilize firms with OSAC/DOS contacts)

• Evaluate terrorist potential, pirate activity, K&R risk, civil unrest, labor strife, etc., for areas of travel

• Ensure GPS tracking system has been installed on vessel so its location can be actively monitored

• Evaluate communication and IT security

• Establish emergency evacuation procedures

• Ensure appropriate medical equipment is on board and crew are trained to use

• Conduct physical security surveys for marina(s) and conduct risk assessment(s) to include policies and procedures, MTSA compliance, backgrounds of marina staff, etc.

• Evaluate overall threat to principal and his/her party and the impact on areas of travel

• Evaluate requirement for security personnel

Aircraft Security

• Identify and confirm the background of all pilots, flight crew and mechanics working on aircraft

• Determine if operating under FAR Part 91 or Part 135 and adhering to recommended TSA security requirements

• Validate all pilot licenses are current and review for FAA sanctions

• Validate they are in possession of a current medical card

• Ensure confidentiality and NDA's are in place

• Conduct periodic TSCM (sweeps) on aircraft to ensure privacy

• Develop a comprehensive written security plan

• Obtain continual and advanced travel itinerary for client and determine risk for each intended location of travel

• Conduct physical security surveys of Fixed Base of Operation (FBO) where aircraft is maintained or areas frequently visited

• Ensure baggage remains in your possession and have a member of flight crew supervise baggage loading

• Identify and screen individuals responsible for the following
  + aircraft cleaning (interior and exterior)
  + aircraft catering
  + aircraft refueling

• Ideally secure aircraft in enclosed hanger with interior security and surveillance system controlled and monitored by owner

Considerations When Selecting an FBO

• Is the airport a controlled or uncontrolled airfield?

• What are the field operating hours?

• What is the access control policy?

• What security procedures are in place to secure the facility?

• Is security staff on site at all times?

• Who has access to aircraft and vehicles?

• What was airport staff turnover percentage in the last year?

• Does perimeter fencing meet TSA security guidelines?

• Is the property patrolled?

• Is there adequate night lighting?

• Are crash/fire/rescue vehicles stationed on site?

• What is the fire department response time?

• Are FAA-compliant background checks performed annually on all personnel with routine access to airport facilities or aircraft?

• Are fingerprints and photos submitted with all background checks?

• Is drug testing regularly performed on all personnel?

• Are all persons with tarmac or aircraft access required to wear photo ID?

• Are security cameras available and in proper working order?

• Are hangars controlled by aircraft owner or FBO?

• Is there fuel farm/truck security?

• Is emergency power available?

• How are aircraft secured?

• How many vehicles are authorized for on-airport use?

• Are unknown vehicles screened and escorted?

• Are drivers screened and licensed?

• Are all vehicles entering parking areas screened?

• Are all parking areas monitored via security cameras?

For the advisor, we suggest that prior to proceeding to the next section, you select one existing client as a benchmark for the aforementioned criteria. Apply the appropriate answers to the lifestyle categories to begin establishing the mosaic of risk based upon your existing knowledge. Take note of what you don't know.

Deliverables – Formulating the Plan

The following criteria are what the affluent client should expect when discussing next steps with their security advisor. This is done after the risk analysis has been completed and the specific threat level has been identified and validated.

1. Probability of risk

Address known, potential and collateral (indirect) risk. These are then evaluated on how they will impact the identified lifestyle vulnerabilities and if sufficient mitigation strategies are deployed through security measures currently in place.

2. Cost

Research all alternatives and always provide options for the client but remember, "cheap is expensive." **Being frugal is prudent— being cheap is dangerous**. Our advice remains constant: Don't spend money unless you have to, but make it an investment and not a cost.

3. Feasibility

Certain solutions may not be feasible for the client despite his or her desire to move in that direction. A prime example is the "Armageddon plan," a doomsday response plan that, in part, calls for 24/7 emergency evacuations from all potential locations regardless of the crisis at hand. Bottom line, it's a great money-maker for a security company but is simply not realistic, and much better solutions are available.

Based upon an understanding of the client's needs and exposures from the above questions, a tailored security plan can now be formulated specific to the individual and family.

CHAPTER
2

SECURING THE HOMEFRONT

From The RCS Files – Florida Home Invasion
In a gated community located in southern Florida, two masked intruders gained entry into an affluent family's home by cutting the glass in a door window, located at the rear of the residence. Once inside, they proceeded to batter the family members (mother, father and daughter), bind them with duct tape and walk the mother into the bedroom where their safe was kept. They then instructed her to open the safe, bag the contents (jewelry and cash) and lie down on her stomach. The intruders were never caught, the property never recovered and the peace inside of their home never regained.

After the case was closed, RCS was brought in to design a new security solution for their home as well as to conduct an investigation into the incident itself. Given the amount of time that had passed, there was virtually nothing that could be done to ascertain the origin. But what did become painfully apparent was the fact that the intruders knew the exact location of the safe. It was additionally determined that the family had recently completed a renovation involving numerous unescorted contractors in their home for more than three months. Furthermore, it was apparent that, during the initial planning of this magnificent $30 million estate, security was spoken about as an afterthought and a rudimentary system (otherwise known as a contractor special) was installed. So not to further exceed the budget, more than the project already had, the contractor skimped on some of the basic requirements expected of a security system to protect such an estate. Clearly one of those cases where, "I'm sorry," simply doesn't work!

The Assessment Process

Perhaps the most critical step in establishing a valid security solution for the affluent client's residence is the risk-assessment process prior to commencing the project. This is where most advisors drop the ball as it is rarely ever done. Hence, the following process should be implemented:

• Conduct a threat analysis on the family by ascertaining what the world knows about them from a comprehensive cyber analysis. When done properly, an individual's wealth, habits, associations, donations and tastes are uncovered. For example, when one acquires an expensive piece of art and has his picture taken with the artwork and is identified by name in the local paper, his address is now easily attainable; we refer to that as an invitation.

• Conducting a risk assessment on the property or location entails garnering both public and nonpublicly available information regarding existing and potential risk to the location. It should be noted that affluent neighborhoods themselves attract skilled intruders and, depending on the precise location, the potential risk can increase exponentially.

• Perform background investigations on all contractors and their personnel. Do not, under any circumstances, ever allow individuals access to your property without thoroughly vetting them. Ask anyone whose sanctity has been violated by someone he has employed, and you will become a believer. Don't roll the dice!

• Establish onsite access control procedures and ensure they are enforced. Bad things happen to good people every day. Protect your human and physical assets by ensuring only those who have been cleared to be on your property are permitted access.

• Ensure all insurance requirements from a security perspective are met. Stay in constant touch with your insurance broker prior to carving out plans with your architect as requirements have been changing rapidly since late 2008. Absent this, the homeowner may be presented with unwanted and unchangeable surprises.

Designing a Layered or Tiered Strategy

The underlying mantra behind the layered security model is to notify the homeowner when an intruder has stepped onto the property, as opposed to after the intruder has gained access to the residence (which is the case in the vast majority of residential security systems). Times have changed, and the traditional burglar alarm of the past, which was designed to protect your possessions when you were away, is not sufficient to protect you and your family while in the residence. Let's crystallize this thought with some germane questions. Looking at the homeowner, how well does he or she respond under extreme stress? How do you feel he or she will respond at 2 a.m. when the alarm is blaring, indicating someone is already in their home? If they intend on defending themselves with a weapon, have they fired the weapon under stressful situations and are they prepared to use deadly force? Have they been counseled about the potential legal ramifications? Hence, it is critical for the advisor to be prepared to discuss this option with their client and for the homeowner to know there are alternatives, such as a tiered strategy, which gives them early notification with sufficient time to secure all family members in a safe room while waiting for law enforcement to respond. This can provide better protection and a far safer solution.

Whether building a home or purchasing an existing one, the home-owner should follow the security system strategy listed below:

• Obtain current site plan

• Conduct thorough background investigations on all contractor personnel to avoid having known criminals and illegal aliens work on your home

• Assess outer perimeter risks (water, woods, public roads and/or unfettered adjoining property access). It is also wise to know who your neighbors are

• Design the outer and inner perimeters of the property.
   + Larger properties – driveway entrance/access gate, etc.
   + Inner perimeter – pool/tennis court access

• Research average local law-enforcement response times

• Consider an intrusion system to include an underground perimeter-sensing cable that provides warning that an intruder has trespassed onto your property long before they reach your front door

• Assess CCTV location for complete coverage to eliminate black-out zones or potential for compromise

• Incorporate appropriate illumination (remember, if you cannot obtain facial recognition, you are wasting your money)

• Ensure proper exterior and interior wiring is installed to include CAT 5, CAT 6 and alarm device cables

• Due to unique specifications and potential difficulty in installation, outdoor cabling requirements must be thoroughly considered prior to construction

• Assess the method of utility wiring from the street poles to your home and consider underground conduit installation to better protect and secure electrical and telephone service

• Evaluate safe room locations, design and potential costs

• Assess lighting requirements (aesthetically pleasing yet productive)

• Have the ability to light up premises inside and out with the flick of a switch

• Ensure all exterior doors and windows are alarmed **properly**

• Ensure inclusion of glass break and motion detection technology and all life safety/environmental devices

• Ensure installation of wireless and hardwired silent panic buttons

• Ensure the alarm panel can integrate the **entire system** for **easy** use

• Ensure that the security alarm system has backup batteries to provide power in the event of a home power loss. It should be noted that it is not uncommon for the more educated intruder to disable power prior to entering the home

• Ensure placement of interior and exterior alarm sounders. Interior sounders should be installed in areas of your home where you may not be able to hear the alarm. Exterior sounders will alert your neighbors and guide the first responders directly to your front door

• Most high-end security system keypads have silent ambush and panic alarm features. Ensure these features are programmed and activated and that you are properly trained in their use

• Ensure that proper backup communications to the alarm panel are in place. Cellular backup will provide communications to the alarm central station in the event that the alarm panel phone lines are cut or tampered with

• Ensure that daily test signals are sent to the central station from the main security alarm panel and the cellular backup alarm panel. These tests should be logged by central station personnel and acted upon in the event a test signal is not received

• Ensure that members of the household and work staff each use a unique ID code to arm and disarm the alarm panel (alarm ID codes should be changed annually) so as to establish and maintain access accountability

• Ensure that the security system is connected to a secure home network with full encryption installed to guard against hacking

• Thoroughly screen the intended alarm/video monitoring company (central station monitoring company contracts must be closely scrutinized)

Prior to Beginning Construction

Once the type of security system is decided upon, it is important to develop a specific security plan for the construction project. The plan is based upon site security assessments, interviews of individuals involved with the project, and an overall risk assessment of the project and its impact on the owners of the property. The purpose of this plan is to minimize the impact of an extraordinary event that could disrupt operations, affect future privacy or security, or seriously impact the financial position or public image of the owners.

All individuals affiliated with the project need to be aware that there is a potential for a variety of situations that could negatively impact the project and, in turn, the owners. It is the responsibility of all subcontractors and other employees to be thoroughly familiarized with this plan. Therefore, all personnel working on the project need to understand that security will not be compromised and violations will jeopardize the opportunity for further employment. This plan needs to be reviewed periodically throughout the project and updated as warranted. The following items should be addressed:

- Access control for employees/contractors/vendors

- Key distribution and tracking

- Badging requirements to allow entry

- Nondisclosure/confidentiality agreement (NDA)

- Locking or securing access points

- Hours of operation

- Visitor policy

- Unauthorized access

- Reporting of security violations and incidents

- Unauthorized items on job site

- Emergency response protocols

- Medical emergency procedures

- Use of electronic surveillance equipment

- Responsibilities of onsite security

- Communications security

- Building plans and document security

- Contractor licensing and insurance

Safe Rooms

Ever since the harrowing film "Panic Room," clients have been having their contractors build safe rooms at a record rate. The concept of safe rooms arose in response to the increased risk of home invasions and kidnapping of affluent individuals and their families. The need to bolster one's security is well understood; however, spending excessive amounts of money on a safe room, without addressing the plethora of related security concerns, is not going to provide the increased level of security desired. A safe room certainly has a place in any comprehensive security plan and needs to be constructed to specific criteria once there is a thorough understanding of pertinent security considerations.

Ideally, the client should meet with a security consultant who reviews the potential risks faced by the individual and the level of existing security measures at the estate. Also, a review of local crime problems should be conducted. Once the level of risk has been determined, the design criteria can be established. Typically an architect is then called in to provide the detail design and documentation of the safe room. The construction design is based upon the level of anticipated risk. The design must also respond to such practical matters as costs and available space.

Safe rooms are not merely a bullet-resistant enclosure. Rather, they are a space offering multiple levels of security designed to meet anticipated threats. They may not necessarily be resistant to all types of attacks. Clearly there may be a difference between the design of a safe room for someone high risk with known threats and that of an individual who may fear some unspecified threat. A modest safe room may be resistant to handguns and physical penetration, whereas a more elaborate safe room may be designed to resist greater ballistic forces as well as require airtight seals to prevent chemical and gas delivery.

To ensure the time necessary to reach a safe room with family members intact, it is imperative that an earlier warning system is in place. If you rely solely on a standard alarm system to notify you of an intrusion, you will have insufficient time to retreat to the safe haven. Perimeter security systems that provide advanced notification when an intruder has entered the property are becoming increasingly popular. The system, which was formally available only to the military and government agencies, will alert the residents, notify law enforcement and also transmit a prerecorded message informing the intruder that they have been detected. This provides sufficient time for the occupants to safely retreat to the safe room location.

The intent is to provide short-term protection for the occupants until help arrives or the attackers leave the scene. In extreme situations, when law enforcement arrives while the criminals are still inside the residence, a hostage/barricade situation may develop. In this scenario, remaining in the safe room for an extended period of time may be required.

Clearly, it is essential that family members can quickly get to the safe room when the potential threat is first detected. Ideally, once the intruder's presence is known, access to the safe room should not require having to confront the attackers in route to its location. Therefore, multiple routes to the safe room are desirable, though not always practical. A location such as a basement in a multi-story residence with only one staircase may be inaccessible from the upper floor bedrooms as the attackers enter the ground level. The occupants, in this case, would have to pass the intruders on the stairs in order to get to the safe room below. This most certainly doesn't work.

Depending on the configuration of the residence, the location for the intended safe room may not be ideal. Oftentimes, it is recommended that several safe rooms be constructed if the interior is not conducive to having one central location from all bedrooms in the house. In larger residences where there are multiple staircases, the issue of location may be less problematic. Where space is not an issue, and there are no budget constraints, a concealed safe room will offer an additional barrier of security for the occupants. These may be located behind a paneled wall where one panel has concealed hinges and locking mechanisms giving access to the protected area on the opposite side. Regardless of the safe room location, it should not be depicted as such on the general building plans. Only those trades required in the construction of the safe room should be provided plans and only on a need-to-know basis.

Safe Room Construction Requirements

Security features of a safe room include bullet-resistant door and walls, sound-proofing, self-contained ventilation system, surveillance cameras and communications equipment. The room is designed and finished around a variety of concealed protective features. The architect plays an important role in disguising the security features to be discreet while integrating them into the overall house design and allowing rapid availability during an emergency.

The following requirements should be taken into consideration for any safe room construction:

• Construction spans floor to ceiling

• Steel stud walls faced with steel sheet and/or bullet-resistant materials such as Kevlar

• Masonry construction may be possible alternative

• Bullet-resistant door with internal steel framing

• Single control point to firmly secure door

• Flame-retardant wall material

• Sound-proofing to muffle noise

• Finish with sheetrock or other decorative finish consistent with the room

• Ceilings constructed similar to walls

• Floors capable of carrying excessive load

• Ensure fresh air intake and exhaust

• Ductwork passing through protected walls needs to protect from poisonous gasses being inserted into the safe room

• Video monitor to access camera system (be sure to locate camera outside safe room)

• Alarm system access

• Multiple communication systems

Additional Accessory Considerations

• Toilet capability

• Flashlights with extra batteries

• Fresh water

• Nonperishable foods

• First aid items

• Gas masks

• Required medication

• Specialized medical equipment

Once the construction is completed, it is imperative emergency drills be held for all occupants so everyone is completely familiar with the safe room operating procedures. Drills should be conducted during daylight and evening hours, without utilizing interior lighting. Do not rely on one primary individual to facilitate the safe room operation since you never know who will be at the residence when it is needed.

CHAPTER
3

COMMUNICATIONS SECURITY

From The RCS Files – Protecting Financial Information
We received a call from a Midwest family distraught over the fact that someone had stolen their identity. This included their bank account numbers, routing information, wire information, PINS and passwords. They advised us that their financial advisor contacted them stating that some unknown person had called their office pretending to be the client and, with all their information in hand, was requesting to close their accounts and move the proceeds. Thanks to a heads-up assistant, the caller was advised that their servers were down and they would have to call him back. When the caller refused to provide a telephone number and insisted he would call back later, the client was alerted immediately. Upon completion of a computer forensics analysis, our investigation revealed that someone had downloaded a key logger on the client's home computer and was consequently monitoring each and every keystroke. The situation was contained, all accounts were

moved, PINS and passwords were changed, cyber security was enhanced and the family was placed on a monthly watch to ensure the thieves would not gain access in the future. However, the fact remains that he still got in and was never apprehended.

The most prevalent 21st century risk to the affluent community is from the cyber criminal. Given the vast amount of information available on the Internet, privacy, or the lack thereof, has taken on a whole new meaning. To really embrace this concept, take a trip down memory lane with us for a moment. Growing up, we used to leave our homes in the morning and return in time for dinner with hands washed and a clean shirt before sitting down to eat. We never once thought to lock the door or close the garage, much less have an alarm system installed. Times were simpler, private property and privacy was respected, and personal information was kept under its respective roof. As time passed, many Americans began to lock their doors (home or not); lock their vehicles, which now have alarm systems as standard equipment; and install residential security systems to the point it has now become the rule, not the exception.

Even more telling, over the past several decades, we have had a metamorphosis of culture as it pertains to how we communicate. For those who remember, our telephones were attached to a cord on the wall, and families had party lines they shared with their neighbors. We have experienced a shift from trying to talk on the phone amidst listening ears in the kitchen to instantaneously communicating with others across the globe with the push of a button.

We have realized tremendous gains and, at the same time, compromised the security of our communications for at least the foreseeable future. Whether we choose to admit it or not, it is incumbent upon each of us to accept a higher level of responsibility over how we communicate over cell phones and on the Internet. However, with respect to the affluent, who possess a significantly higher probability of risk from the hacking constituency, incorporating communication-security best practice measures is a must. Therefore, it is imperative for the advisor to assist his or her clients by evaluating their communications security practices and implementing the required solutions.

However, prior to implementing a plan, the advisor must first understand the baseline of risk that presents itself to the affluent client.

Keep in mind the concept of negative migration: Negative behavior migrates to the path of least resistance. Few things are more important to remember than this truth because it embodies the very essence of preparedness required by each affluent client as well as their advisors. In spirit, nothing is impenetrable, which is why it is not the job of the advisor to create such a solution. Moreover, the true goal is to implement a communications security strategy that will be secure enough to force the intruder to move on to the next person who has prepared far less and is a less difficult target. The bottom line is that the easier clients make it for the hacking community to break into their lives, the more vulnerable they will remain, which is why best practices must be incorporated.

Best practices call for the following measures:

- Do not leave your computer unattended when you are logged on

- Do not leave your password anywhere close to your computer

- Change passwords frequently

- Control access to your computers and backups

- Be sure to log off when done with the computer

- Maintain an appropriate level of protection for all laptop computers by remembering the following:
    + Provide appropriate protection and security at your residence
    + Never leave a laptop in plain view inside a vehicle
    + Never leave a laptop unattended anywhere, for any length of time. This includes airports, train and bus stations, vehicles, meeting rooms, hotels, etc.

- Never check in a laptop computer as luggage

• Ensure all critical information is backed up and maintained in a secure location.

• Install a dedicated server within the home to act as the communication brain. For the affluent client, this calls for a step above the typical firewall solution, which houses standard algorithms that more experienced hackers can bypass easily

• Integrate all house phones (preferably VOIP), cell phones, security systems and Internet connection through the server

• Monitor system with comprehensive event logging.

Here's the litmus test of whether this applies to you:

1. Do you bank online?

2. Do you trade stocks online?

3. Do your children go online? Do they participate in social networking sites?

4. Do your children participate in gaming online?

5. Do you email family pictures?

6. Do you shop online?

7. Do you email personal information?

If you answer "yes" to any of the above questions, seek assistance in developing comprehensive communication security protocols. This is a must!

Refer to the Smart Home Network Architecture Questionnaire in Appendix A.

Chapter
4

Protecting Your Children

Simply put, there is no greater asset in life than your children, so not incorporating the highest level of protection around them is, without question, inexcusable. In the unfortunate event that children perish as a result of a situation that may have been avoided, the heart-wrenching anguish that develops lives with parents and family members forever. Yet, for some very bizarre reason, it is commonplace for affluent parents to hire employees charged with the task of caring for their children (such as nannies) and other household staff without a thorough background investigation ever being conducted. Additionally, contractors, who have also never been screened, are consistently permitted access inside and outside the residence.

This mistake was nearly memorialized when the young son of a well-known business personality was nearly abducted by a convicted sex offender while employed as a contract painter at the person's residence. This, of course, begs the question: How many more times must we experience these situations before protecting children becomes of paramount concern to parents? Of all the matters we manage on a daily basis, this is by far the most confusing and perplexing. As will be discussed in greater detail in the next section, there is a gross disparity between the quintessential nanny check and a thorough background investigation. As for this critical subject, absent the thorough background investigation, access to your children should be avoided for all those who would be permitted direct (e.g. nanny) or indirect (e.g. landscaper) contact with your children.

The following standalone sources are red flags that should be avoided in this process:

• Referrals from friends or acquaintances (apologies don't suffice post-incident)

• Internet/newspaper advertisements (this is not where you find the right people)

• Employment/placement agencies whom you assume are thoroughly vetting prospects

• Foreign-born individuals without written proof of legal alien status (look up USC Title 8, § 1324, and ask yourself if going to jail for five years is an option you want to consider)

• Self-initiated backgrounds (if it's not what you do for a living, don't experiment with your children)

Oftentimes we can make some minor lifestyle modifications to increase security and safety for our children. The following security precautions can be easily implemented.

Family Security/Safety Measures

• Lose the vanity plates (no reason to drive you and your children around in a vehicle that can be easily recognized or remembered)

• Be aware of any strangers loitering on street corners or around the neighborhood

• Note vehicles that are often parked up the street but still have line of sight to the residence

• Take down suspicious license plate numbers and description of the vehicle and occupants

• Note vehicles that seem to cruise the neighborhood

• Do not open the door to anyone unless the person is positively identified

• Do not tell strangers, shopkeepers or tradesmen about family travel plans

• Families should avoid consistent travel patterns when working, shopping or attending social activities

• When planning a trip, do not stop services and deliveries but rather let friends or staff members handle these matters during your absence

• Do not jog or walk near the home at the same time each day

• Make certain that outside doors are secured and alarm set when both at home and away from residence

• Never leave young children at home unattended

• Instruct caregivers to keep the doors and windows locked and to never let in strangers

• Teach children as early as possible how to call the police should strangers or prowlers loiter around the house or attempt to gain entry

• Keep the house well lit when you are at home

• Avoid obvious indications that your home is unattended or absent adults (e.g., garage doors left open with no vehicles inside)

From The RCS Files – Holiday Suicide Avoided
It was just about 5:30 p.m. on the evening before a holiday when the call came into the RCS hot line. A distraught mother advised that her teenage son had left home earlier in the day driving the family van. He was emotionally upset, despondent and possibly suicidal. She felt strongly that he would in all likelihood take his life that evening if he were not found. She stated that she had contacted the police earlier, but there was little they would do at this point based upon the limited information regarding the individual's current whereabouts. Using information provided, RCS was able to deploy investigators to areas that the youth frequents and develop critical intelligence about his whereabouts. Within four hours, a RCS investigator had located the youth, who had registered at a local hotel. Once inside the room, a suicide note was found, leading investigators to the rooftop of the building, where the teenager was talked down from jumping and taking his life.

Managing substance abuse and family mergers are perhaps two of the most challenging subjects the advisor will be confronted with in serving the affluent client. Therefore, it is incumbent upon the advisor to screen and secure a best in practice mental health provider who can provide exemplary and expeditious service to the family regardless of venue.

Also of concern is the importance of having a family relocation and communications plan. The protocols to follow in the event of an emergency situation need to be understood and agreed upon by all family members. There were a high number of school age children stranded after 9/11 since their parents were faced with road closures and unable to get to the schools and pick them up. These children had no concept of what to do when their parents did not arrive, and the schools had no plan in place to best care for students until parents could get there. (In New York City, this was days, in some cases!) Parents are urged to contact their children's schools and verify that they have developed specific plans to address emergency situations, including national disasters.

Stress the importance of family members knowing what to do if you can't contact one another by phone and where to gather in an emergency. Most likely, if we are the victim of another terrorist attack, the U.S. government will immediately cut off or restrict cell phone service in specific areas since this is the preferred communication source used by terrorists and is often the way that their bombs are detonated. We all need a plan that is easy enough for even our youngest children to remember and follow.

As previously discussed, the Internet has brought great advantages and disadvantages to our way of life. Specifically, mitigating potential risks to the affluent community and their children is an ongoing concern and one the advisor must be prepared to offer counsel.

The following are the most prudent recommendations:

• Limit or monitor participation in social networking sites

• Refrain from electronically sending personal pictures

• Monitor any Internet gaming

• Educate children on the messages they send via email, text or instant messages, as they are often misused

• Consider installing a family-based server within the home that provides enhanced security for desktop and laptop computers

• Install disc-level encryption and GPS tracking on all the laptop computers

• Limit Internet purchases to known sites and use a separate credit card with a low limit for these transactions only

• Consider biometric or facial recognition software to control unauthorized access to laptops

For example, a young teenage boy was an avid Xbox user, playing games with cyber friends all over the country via the Internet. He became online friends with "Michael," who purported to be a 13-year-old boy from New York City. In reality, he was a 42-year-old convicted pedophile. Through online conversations, they agreed to meet in person on a Saturday afternoon in the city.

Fortunately for the intended victim, the FBI's Cyber Unit was also monitoring the gaming site and was able to intervene. Instead of the pedophile meeting with his intended victim, he was arrested. Though a tragedy was narrowly avoided, the unfortunate fact of this whole situation is that the parents were completely unaware of what their son was doing and the fact he had developed "cyber friends." Being oblivious to your children's activities is a recipe for disaster.

School Security

With an increase in school-related incidents involving both students and teachers, it is incumbent that a certain amount of due diligence be performed prior to sending a child off to school. From daycare and preschool to K-12 and boarding school, selecting the safest location with a thoroughly vetted staff is a must. Specifically, the following measures should be examined by the affluent client prior to finalizing a decision on school selection:

- Physical security measures in place

- Access control to campus and buildings

- Review of emergency response plans and procedures

- Visitor sign-in policy and escort procedures

- Staff background investigations

- Student sign-out policy

- Security measures in place to protect personal information

- A grid search of surrounding areas to identify local crime problems and identify any registered sex offenders in close proximity

- View website to ensure students are not identified by name and or picture

College Security Concerns

We find ourselves reading all too frequently of the tragedies impacting our children at major universities and colleges: the mass shooting at an East Coast university leaving 32 dead and dozens wounded; the abduction and subsequent murder of a coed at an Ivy League university; and the near-fatal stabbing by a scorned lover in the lab at a major California university in front of 30 witnesses. These are all examples of the violence on our campuses that is showing no signs of being eliminated. These risks cannot be completely avoided; however, we can do our research to ensure the schools that our sons or daughters are attending adhere to required security standards.

The Jeanne Clery Act, USC Title 20, § 1092(f), is the landmark federal law, originally known as the Campus Security Act, that requires colleges and universities across the United States to disclose information regarding crime statistics on and around their campuses. It also requires them to provide a description of the type and frequency of security measures and the programs available to inform students about campus security procedures and practices.

Because the law is tied to participation in federal student financial aid programs, it applies to most institutions of higher education both public and private and is enforced by the U.S. Department of Education. Subsequent amendments as recent as 2008 added provisions pertaining to registered sex offender notification and campus emergency response procedures. It is imperative that school security measures, as evaluated through the Jeanne Clery Act, are part of the decision-making process when selecting a college or university to attend.

Other considerations include:

• Does the campus implement best practices regarding physical security?

• Is there a campus police force or security deployed on a 24/7 basis?

• Is access controlled to campus, dorms and classrooms?

• Is there a student body notification system in the event of an emergency?

• Are there adequate emergency response procedures with documented plans?

• Are emergency drills conducted?

• How is the faculty and service staff vetted?

• Are there adequate security measures in place to protect students' personal information?

• Conduct a grid search to identify the crime problems adjacent to the property and registered sex offenders.

• View website to ensure students are not identified by name and or picture

Housing

Many considerations go into determining where the student will live once living at home is no longer an option. For the student living in the dorm, they are most likely assigned a roommate whom they may know nothing about. Depending on the school, the dorms may be coed, further increasing exposure and potential concerns. Access controls to the facility need to be closely examined, as well as other security measures previously discussed. Most schools have certain security protocols in place; however, these need to be examined and fully vetted to ensure policies are strictly enforced.

Most importantly, the student needs to be educated about his or her potential as a target and to be cautious when meeting new people. They cannot show up at orientation driving a brand new, expensive vehicle parked in front for all to see. Or once at school, they can't display the ability to have a continual supply of money and nice things. They will attract individuals who want to befriend them merely to share in the financial benefit of being around them. Buying concert tickets, going to restaurants, borrowing money (with no intention of repaying), using their vehicle, and other items can certainly attract "new friends" for all the wrong reasons. Others may be attracted for far more sinister reasons and actually target them for abduction, blackmail or extortion for a much larger payday.

If the student is going to live off campus, a suitable residence must be identified with the ability to implement sufficient security measures. Many families choose to buy a townhouse or rent an apartment close to campus for their student to live. Ideally, if this is going to be a purchase, ensure it does not identify the family or student which could red flag them as having money. Consider conducting a security assessment on any identified residence for a student prior to purchasing or renting.

The assessment should include the following:

- Evaluate neighborhood crime problems

- Proximity to street

- Identify potential neighbors

- Background potential roommates

- Evaluate street lighting

- Parking availability

- Proximity to campus and ability to walk or bike

- Entry points to property

- Key accountability

- Security measures in place

- Ability to upgrade security

- Fire system

- Law enforcement response time

- If ground floor location, what types of windows and doors

- Emergency evacuation route

- IT/communications security

From The RCS Files – Making New Friends
The student just returned home from college with his "new friend." He appeared like any other freshman college student, and he was well-mannered, polite and respectful. The parents, being the gracious hosts they are, welcomed their son's new friend with open arms. In fact, they stated they were so pleased he had found a new friend who appeared so nice. Within several days, he knew the alarm code, gate code and where the spare key was hidden, and he had been given a complete tour that had pointed out valuable artwork, irreplaceable memorabilia and jewelry locations.

The family was preparing to go on a ski trip and asked the new friend to accompany them. He stated he needed to go home to visit his parents and declined the offer. A few days later, the family departed and, upon their return, discovered they were the victims of a residential burglary.

Investigation quickly placed the "new friend" at the top of the suspect list. Upon initial questioning, the family could not even recall the state where the student stated he lived. Contact with the school determined no one by that name had ever been enrolled as a student. It was later determined the "new friend" was actually a 25-year-old con man wanted in multiple states.

Studying Abroad

Study abroad programs can be an exciting time for a student and provide him or her with multiple layers of education. However, it can also present significant risk, which is why the advisor must be prepared to guide the affluent client through the process.

Some suggestions are as follows:

• Ensure the institution has conducted thorough background investigations on supervising staff

• Ensure due diligence has been conducted on the host site, including housing arrangements

• Ensure thorough and frequent student welfare checks are conducted and contact numbers provided

• Ensure crisis contingency plans have been formulated to include medical assistance and evacuation procedures and that they include notification procedures

• Country-specific education addressing the various cultures must be provided to the student in advance

• Provide U.S. State Department your contact information while in foreign countries

Remember, embracing the aforementioned procedures regarding your children does not make you paranoid—it makes you prepared!

Chapter
5

INTEGRITY VALIDATION

From The RCS Files – Extortion Scheme
Having been retained by a family in the Northeast to conduct background investigations on their household staff (after a significant theft had occurred), we learned that the property manager of 10 years had an extensive criminal history and had been charging a tariff from all subcontractors in order for them to keep their service contracts with the family. Further investigation revealed that the subject had made a number of extravagant purchases, including land where he was planning to build a new residence—all of which far exceeded his means based upon his declared income. After briefing the client, they decided not to pursue it further to avoid public embarrassment and to discharge him immediately. Years later, new employee selection protocols are in place, but the sense of betrayal and personal violation remains.

Unfortunately, many high-net-worth clients have realized the need to conduct thorough background investigations only after being victimized. With billions of dollars lost to fraudulent schemes every year, the advisor must be prepared to guide the client through this process so that the information he or she receives is both pertinent and reliable.

It is important to conduct background investigations on all household employees and advisors, with updates conducted a minimum of every year. Trusted individuals repeatedly violate families' trust due to outside pressures and vices such as gambling, alcohol or drug abuse. Oftentimes, changes in behavior are also associated with the death of a family member or loved ones, divorce, bad decision-making or one spouse losing his or her job. All can negatively impact the individual's household finances and result in them turning to drastic measures that normally would never be considered.

What Is a Comprehensive Background?

A sampling of the background information that should be examined as a minimum in each venue is as follows:

• Character, reputation and integrity of individual

• Criminal and civil litigation history in local, state and federal courts

• Education verification

• Prior job history verification

• Verification of licenses required for employment

• Address history

• Credit history

• Bankruptcy/liens/judgments

- Sexual predator list

- Watch list (global criminal)

As a matter of business protocol, the results of these inquiries must be analyzed by experienced personnel who have extensive investigative experience in identifying "red flags" and who can provide appropriate recommendations to address each and every potential concern revealed. This is not an exercise in transferring information from public databases onto company letterhead but gleaning and analyzing behavioral intelligence on individuals to provide a valid portrait of the intended hire.

Typical Situations Requiring This Course of Action:

- Hiring/retaining household staff

- Selecting/retaining professional advisors

- Hiring/retaining vendors/contractors

- Hiring/retaining yacht/aircraft crew

- Hiring/retaining family office staff

- Entering into new business ventures with unknown individuals

- Potential new spouse prior to marriage into affluent family

You must provide a written release form to be signed by the applicant prior to the pre-employment investigation being conducted. The applicant is able to question the accuracy of the report and must be given the opportunity to do so. There are legal limitations on how far back information can be researched on an individual. Notifying the applicant that a search for criminal records will be part of the background oftentimes will discourage applicants who have something to hide; however, only convictions and pending cases can be considered.

When a background investigation is conducted, it should be done under the auspices of federal Fair Credit Reporting Act (FCRA). Many states also have their own rules, which can add additional legal requirements. The essential thrust of the FCRA is that an applicant must specifically authorize the background investigation in writing. The applicant must also receive a disclosure concerning his or her rights.

Background investigations should also include a credit report. A credit report is just one type of consumer report that can be used in addition to criminal records, educational verifications and other background tools. Credit reports are more sensitive and should be treated with special precautions.

False information and outright lies on employment applications are much more common than most believe. Job applicants falsely list years of education, experience, training and neglect to state prior criminal histories. They often believe they will not be found out by the employer, and, if a firm specializing in this type of work is not retained, most likely, they are right.

Upon reviewing case law, it appears that the burden on the employer to show they have performed "reasonable" due diligence has been increased, and the failure to perform, or if performed in a negligent manner, could prove to be very costly. It seems that the burden has also increased from a mere database check, which has been the norm and perhaps the accepted practice, to requiring comprehensive checks of civil and criminal records. Another concern is that research cannot be limited to the current place of residency but must include all counties where the individual lived, was previously employed and places where the applicant spent a considerable amount of time, such as school, summer activities and travel.

The real issue becomes "what is reasonable." For a background investigation to be complete and thorough, it must utilize a variety of proprietary databases only available to licensed investigators. We are beginning to see the $99 Internet inquiry becoming a thing of the past. Those who rely on the Internet, without personal contact and knowledge of credentials, are placing themselves at risk as far as liability is concerned. Background investigation companies offering personal services, with certified credentials, will soon become the norm and not the exception.

Prior to hiring or investing with any new company, making philanthropic donations or making other business decisions involving unknown individuals, conduct the following research as a standard course of practice.

Business Background Requirements

- Extensive research on the firm and its principals

- Prior bankruptcies

- Liens/judgments

- Corporations filings

- Proper licensing

- Business filings in state(s) doing business

- UCC filings

- Associated businesses and principals

- Internet domain names registered to business

- Current and previous property ownership

- Current motor vehicles registered to individual

- Dun & Bradstreet report

- Better Business Bureau

Conducting Interviews

Oftentimes after the initial background investigation is complete, further information or clarification is required prior to hiring the individual. The art of interviewing requires a proven process to ensure you are obtaining factual information to reach the proper decision. For key hires, be certain you have an experienced interviewer who can easily step into the role of interrogator if inconsistent or misleading information is provided. The following interview techniques can assist in conducting a successful interview:

- Thoroughly prepare for the interview
  + Methodical review of application
  + Consider communication barriers such as language, culture, gender, emotions, etc.

- Establish control, rapport and credibility with individual

- Don't ask too many questions initially

- Convince individual to be straightforward

- Don't allow theme of questioning to shift

- Determine if direct or indirect questions are best, based upon the personality of individual

- Ask leading questions, which contain the answers or a choice of answers

- Be continually alert for inconsistencies in answers

- Practice active listening

- Don't interrupt or finish other person's sentence

- Continually monitor nonverbal communication
  + Eye contact, body movement, voice pitch, facial expressions,

gestures and verbal content

- At termination of the interview, ask, "Is there anything else I didn't ask or anything you want to add?" (We have learned much from this technique.)

CHAPTER
6

Safeguarding the Family Office

Perhaps the fastest-growing business segment in the United States, the family office has become both an invaluable resource for the affluent family and a significant source of vulnerability to their legacy. The office is relied upon to provide services ranging from managing investments and legal matters to conducting personal shopping and hiring household staff. This rapidly growing entity is faced with significant challenges, considering the overt exposure that is generated by the family's wealth. Managed properly, this business unit can provide substantial assistance to the family in preserving or safeguarding current assets and optimizing future gains. However, if the appropriate internal controls are not implemented, the family office can become a platform for the 21st century intruder to feed from. In essence, in serving its constituency, a clearinghouse of information is created that, if compromised, can devastate a family for life. The following anecdotes will help to crystallize this point.

A senior executive for a single-family office (SFO) in the Northwest was on business travel and had his laptop stolen from the hotel room. Unfortunately, he failed to install the appropriate level of encryption on his computer, and the identities of all 38 family members were compromised, along with their bank account and tax information. Needless to say, his employment was terminated, and the family members remain on a monthly monitoring program after having endured more than a dozen subsequent attempts of identity theft.

A receptionist for a multiple family office (MFO) on the West Coast spent more than five years making unapproved withdrawals from various family accounts before her efforts were uncovered. Given the fact that the MFO did not conduct a data classification exercise and implement decentralized electronic access, all employees were able to view (as well as manipulate) all available client information. The MFO closed its doors shortly thereafter, and the whereabouts of the receptionist remain unknown.

At a SFO in the Southeast, an employee charged with the task of managing all the family's real estate concerns was preparing for his retirement by creating sidebar financial relationships (kickbacks) with more than 300 contractors. Their financial advisor became suspicious when, shortly before the employee's last day, they received an alarming phone call from a former contractor that prompted an investigation. After several weeks, it was revealed that the employee had been receiving kickbacks for more than three years. Wanting to avoid further public disclosure, the family terminated the employee and refrained from legal action. Needless to say, their position on vetting employees prior to hiring has changed drastically.

Due to the significant increase in the family office being used as a holistic resource for the management of the affluent community, our family office clients and colleagues repeatedly requested a blueprint in which they could self-assess their respective security posture. As a result, the RCS Family Office Certification Program was created to provide this business sector with the roadmap to evaluating operational, physical, systems, financial, travel and personal security protocols through an established process of related controls. Since risks evolve over time, particularly as personnel and technology change, it is important to conduct a formal risk assessment, as further discussed in this chapter, every couple of years to ensure controls are focused in the right areas.

Internal controls are the processes and procedures that a family office uses to build security and integrity into all its critical functions. A solid framework of internal controls is essential to risk management, which protects family wealth and provides an operational structure that the office can rely on as it continues to grow and prosper. Internal controls will not prevent every problem or occurrence of fraud, but they will discourage inconsistency and unreliability in the management of the family's affairs.

We can all remember the security measures that were immediately put in place post 9/11. Vehicles were screened for explosive devices, magnetometers were installed in every major office building, purses and briefcases were hand-searched and security guards were prevalent everywhere. Then, in the matter of a few short months, they were gone. Now, few truly embraced the excessive security measures that impacted us all; however, we appreciated it less when everything was abruptly removed. Especially since we were gearing up for the war in Iraq, terrorist groups were still threatening our homeland, and we had not apprehended the masterminds of the U.S. attacks. The cause for removal was motivated on nothing more than financial reasons. The problem is that the security measures imposed were excessive in most areas, absent direct threats, and, overall, they were not sustainable or long-term solutions.

The significance of this lesson is to understand the importance in developing a security program that is sustainable and acceptable to all family members. The family must fully comprehend and embrace the requirements of a comprehensive security program and set the bar at an acceptable level that can be easily raised in the event unforeseen situations dictate. Once it is determined that security needs to be elevated—due to current situations such as stalking, death threats or an increase in area home invasions—it is maintained at that level for the duration. Once the crisis passes, security is then reduced to the established baseline and never below. As life-altering situations occur, security needs to be re-evaluated to ensure an adequate baseline is maintained.

Family office members may innocently create a security risk to the family when they have access to critical family information and are actively involved in the family office operation. It is imperative everyone operates under a cloak of operational security and shares information strictly on a "need to know" basis. The following rules summarize the principal issues inherent to effective operational security:

• Set the tone. Demonstrate that everyone needs to be sensitive to security issues. This "tone at the top" also is a key driver for developing an office culture of security awareness and behavior.

• Develop a family office security plan. Craft a plan to ensure everyone's safety and accountability along with contingency planning if an incident were to occur.

• Be aware of surroundings. Look for and respond to suspicious activity or unusual behavior. More information has been lost through email, simple overhears, phone contacts, "pretext" interviews and other social engineering techniques than through exotic electronic devices.

• Be an active participant. It's better to report unremarkable activity than allow a material risk to go unnoticed. Challenge friends and acquaintances who are seeking confidential or personal family information.

• Ensure you know who will receive faxed information prior to sending. Do not fax travel itineraries or proprietary information unless the intended recipient is available at the fax machine to receive the document. Ideally, scan all information and send via email through secure server.

• Silence is golden. Never discuss confidential matters in a public setting or on an analog cellular or cordless phone. This includes email from non-encrypted servers.

• Remain hands-on. Keep personal control of confidential information. Do not leave confidential material unattended at work, in a vehicle, in your home or hotel room.

• Don't give it away. Do not discard confidential materials without shredding in a confetti-cut shredder

The following information takes a page out of our family office play book. It is presented to the executive to crystallize the depth of this initiative and further illustrate the value of conducting such an exercise for the family office to assure the security of its family's name, wealth and legacy. We encourage you to evaluate your current security posture.

Operational Security

• Are security policies and procedures in place, such as access control, visitor escorting, document security and communications security?

• Are HR policies compliant and enforced to avoid employment law issues?

• Is a security training and operational awareness program in place for both office and house staff?

• Are thorough background investigations conducted on employees and contractors prior to hiring for the office and the families' homes?

• Are disaster recovery (DR) plans documented and DR exercises conducted on a yearly basis to test systems for failsafe preparedness?

• Are nondisclosure/integrity assurance agreements in place for all employees and contractors?

• In protecting family information from theft and extortion, are technical surveillance countermeasure (TSCM) inspections periodically conducted?

• Is investigative due diligence conducted for family members prior to committing monies to investments or donations?

• Is the family name protected from unneeded exposure on the Internet?

• Are crisis preparedness and response plans in place to protect the family in the event of exposure to such issues as kidnap for ransom, extortion, stalking, child abduction, home invasion, hate crimes and terrorist attacks?

Physical Security Requirements

• Are access controls in place for all external ingress/egress points?

• Should bulletproof glass be installed in the principal's office?

• Are strategically installed CCTV cameras installed in all critical areas?

• Are all critical IT systems integrated within an encrypted server and appropriately protected through the use of software and hardware devices?

• Has glass-break technology been strategically installed within the offices where appropriate?

• Are all exterior electrical and communications cabinets locked and monitored for breach?

• Are fire control detection systems in a secured area?

• Is confidential trash properly disposed of to insure destruction?

• Are controlled access procedures in place for cleaning crews, contractors and maintenance personnel or are they permitted unfettered access to the office when no one is there?

• Are families' homes professionally secured in relation to the exposure their wealth creates (see chapter on Securing the Home Front)?

Systems Security

• Is a qualified patch management process in place for all workstations and servers?

• What type of user identification, authentication and authorization process controls are in place throughout the environment?

• Are application security controls in place?

• Are wireless network access points necessary? If they are, are they appropriately protected with the latest authentication mechanisms?

• Are sensitive data exchanges secured and are data classification levels on critical databases enforced?

• Are data or email encryption technologies in place to protect sensitive information leaving your server and desktop environments?

• Are intrusion prevention controls in place across the network?

• Are the NAC (network access control) hardware and policies valid and reliable?

• Is the firewall administration outsourced?

• Are there any types of intrusion detection system (IDS) or intrusion prevention systems (IPS) present?

• Are incident response procedures currently in place?

• Are procedures—including appliance and device documentation—documented and provided for secure, off-site storage?

• Are response methods (i.e., battery back-up times, recovery timelines for critical systems, equipment and data back-ups, etc.) in sync with expectations of management?

• Are network administration capabilities controlled by only qualified network administrators?

• Are network administrators monitored for their activity? Does executive management maintain a separate administrative user name/password, or does the IT manager have the "keys to the kingdom?"

• Are regular, external IT security audits conducted to ensure level of security measures are appropriately in place and operational?

• Are IT protocols in place and exercised when employees are terminated (i.e., downloaded and archived email profiles, user access terminated, etc.)?

Travel Protocols

• Are travel itineraries protected and are travel agents thoroughly screened?

• Is investigative due diligence conducted prior to the acquisition of aircrafts and yachts, and are TSCM inspections conducted prior to travel by new owners?

• Are personal protection protocols in place?

• Are risk assessments conducted on each venue prior to family members traveling and reports generated for family review?

• Are contingency plans in place to assist family members while traveling, in the event an emergency evacuation is required?

• Are children/young adults traveling without adult escort educated on the risks of abduction and general safety protocols?

Personal Security Awareness

Are appropriate family members (including children) provided security awareness information and seminars on the following topics?

• Stalking

• Identity theft

• Kidnap for ransom (to include express kidnap scenarios)

• Extortion

• Safe dating

• Travel awareness

• Child protection

• Self-defense

• Adverse media containment

Financial Controls

In a first-generation family office, the patriarch, matriarch or other designated family leader usually plays an active role in overseeing family affairs and safeguarding family assets. He or she works closely with the staff and often has sole check-signing authority. As the family office grows, this oversight role shifts to trusted employees or governing boards.

In addition to all the risk-mitigation strategies previously stated, financial controls must ensure the preservation of current assets and optimization of future gains. They must also be consistent with the family's tolerance for risk. Policies should be developed to address day-to-day transactional matters, investment management and performance measurement guidelines. The following topics should be addressed:

- Fund transfers

- Bookkeeping/reconciliation protocols

- Protection from unauthorized investment transactions

- Authorizations/limits/access: procedures that safeguard access to funds

- Improper allocation of investment funds

- Recording cash receipts

- Disbursements

- Payroll controls to eliminate fraud: ghost employees

- Segregation of duties: investments, financial accounting, reporting

During these challenging economic times, the family office must increase awareness regarding the potential for fraud, specifically involving readily accessible cash and the family's investment portfolio. Additional monitoring measures and controls may be prudent to cover multiple risks, not just those associated with, say, stocks or bonds. Performance expectations based upon independent research, benchmark performance in today's climate and good old reliance on common sense (the greatest oxymoron of all time) should all be part of infusing new controls into the family office corporate culture.

Whether you are a SFO caring for one multigenerational family or a MFO responsible for the well-being of numerous families, there are several underlying questions. How secure of an environment have you created for those that have bestowed you with their family trust? What is your margin for error in protecting this trust? Moreover, what is critical for you to remember is that organized crime groups such as the Russian Mafia, Triad and the FARC (to name a few) are extremely well equipped and funded to explore all potential avenues into the lives of the affluent. Given the significant return on investment that can be realized in concert with the typical ideology of "My families aren't celebrities, so risk is low," the family office entity makes the perfect setting for one-stop criminal shopping. If you remove the emotional side of this equation and look at it as they do, this is a prime business venture. Therefore, we beseech you: Do not think this can't happen to you!

A final anecdote for your consideration

A large single-family office with members located all over the United States was charged with the task of overseeing the renovation of a home in excess of 30,000 square feet. More than 75 percent through the project, it became apparent that certain contractors were falsifying manpower reports and submitting highly questionable invoices, which prompted a thorough investigation into the billing process. No family representative had been hired to oversee the construction project, and the contractor did not have the financial sophistication to track accurate payments of invoices. Upon completion of the investigation, the family office client was advised not to pay any of the outstanding invoices and to close down the site until background investigations could be completed on all contractors. It was determined that more than 35 percent of those previously permitted on the job site were convicted felons or currently had outstanding warrants. To add insult to injury, the architectural plans, which were displayed throughout the job site, bore the clients' name, security system design and camera locations. Shortly after moving in, they were victimized by a home invasion.

Chapter 7

TRAVEL SECURITY

From The RCS Files – Medivac from Latin America

At the request of a client, we conducted a travel intelligence analysis of a Latin American country prior to their daughter's trip to identify any potential concerns. Upon completion, we advised the client that there were no immediate threats but that this particular country had a reputation of being non- cooperative with U.S. interests and citizens in the past. Given the daughter's health condition and the lack of adequate medical facilities available, in concert with the prevailing attitude toward U.S. citizens, we advised against the trip.

However, not wanting to disappoint their daughter, she was given the required spending money and sent off. Several days later, our client telephoned us through our call center at approximately 2:30 a.m. in a frantic state. Her daughter, who, due to her medical condition, is not permitted to consume alcohol, did just that and became extremely ill.

Without proper medical care available, they attempted to have their aircraft (with the family doctor on board) pick her up and return her home. Unfortunately, the foreign government would not allow them to do so prior to a 72-hour time period due to visa requirements, which prompted the mother's call to RCS. We immediately began looking for an alternative solution to improve the medical situation while negotiations to land in-country were initiated. After learning further of the victim's medical condition, we were able to determine that the fact she was at an elevation over 8,000 feet was compounding her situation.

We arranged to have her transported to a lower elevation, where her condition immediately improved. RCS professionals were able to contact associates in the subject country and arranged for the plane to land at a specified airstrip to pick up the daughter and depart immediately. Regardless of the destination, obtaining travel intelligence and establishing preemptive contingency plans is more than prudent, it is essential.

Precautions for the International Traveler

The easiest way to grasp the importance of assessing the degree of risk prior to traveling abroad is for all those intending to engage in such a venture to accept that kidnap and ransom is a billion-dollar business, and the affluent traveler is the commodity. The individual's identity, organizational affiliations and numerous other factors will determine his or her worth to the kidnappers or extortionists. Therefore, obtaining proper intelligence prior to venturing overseas is absolutely necessary for the affluent individual.

Since 1970, a number of political terrorist groups have used kidnapping to obtain ransom money to fund terrorist organizations. It is difficult to ascertain the accurate number of annual international kidnappings; however, they are believed to be substantially higher than in the U.S. and may exceed 10,000 per year. Studies show that ransom demands domestically average approximately $1 million in comparison to $10 million or more in other parts of the world. Wealthy North American travelers, who can be easily identified from the Internet, have been targeted in many of these kidnappings, which have taken place worldwide over the past 20 years. Be aware, there is a strong correlation between an individual's level of income and notoriety and their likelihood of becoming a kidnap victim.

Affluent Americans are perceived to be vast repositories of wealth, and have unwillingly been placed at risk. They are faced with the challenges of embracing a new level of responsibility to their families, as well as to their employees, during the ongoing war on terror. Clearly, the greatest challenge as it relates to travel and personal security will be to proactively address the increased potential for kidnapping.

Given the fact that terrorist cells are now operating under a decentralized decision-making structure, continued funding is a primary agenda item. That said, the omnipresent threat evident to the affluent community and corporate executives from kidnap and ransom scenarios have and will continue to increase dramatically. Affluent individuals and their families are viewed as powerful commodities, and cell leaders recognize this as a substantial source for generating revenue.

Utilization of a private aircraft will significantly lessen vulnerability from kidnapping when traveling. This specifically allows the ability to avoid public airports and not travel on a pre-determined schedule to coincide with scheduled flights. However, while on the ground, security of the aircraft is an important consideration and needs to be included in the overall travel security plan.

Recommendations for Safe Travel

During perhaps the most tumultuous times in recent history, ensuring safe travel for the affluent is of paramount concern. It is with this in mind that the adage "Proper Planning Avoids Panic and Paranoia" rings true.

Regardless of the mode of travel, traveling domestically or internationally presents inherent risks if due caution is not exercised. Travel security within the U.S. generally presents lower risk levels than traveling to international markets. However, concerns from kidnap and ransom, blackmail, robbery and other threats to personal safety are prevalent in the U.S. as well as abroad. It is incumbent upon us all to re-examine the manner in which we plan our travel, the precautions we take while traveling, our mind-set regarding safety upon arrival at our destination and the distinction between domestic and international travel risks.

Given the apparent risks and the need for peace of mind, consider implementing the following recommendations to enhance personal safety during travel.

Pre-Travel Planning

• Limit travel itinerary to a "need to know" basis and delegate someone as a 24/7 contact and arrange daily communication protocol

• Every traveler should have a system of accountability for tracking family members while traveling. This information must be limited to involved parties only and never discussed outside that inner circle

• Provide prearranged car service submitting segments of travel only

• Ensure no signs are presented to identify the individual traveling by name at the airport.

• Identify alternative routes of travel, including different modes of transportation, to provide prompt response in the event of a crisis

• Select a separate credit card to be used for all travel reservations and accommodations

• Make copies of wallet contents and passport/visa prior to travel

• Ensure all required medication is packed in carry-on bags

• Remove all forms of identification from travel bags by substituting them with other identifying features.

There is no reason to advertise who you are or where you live. One alternative is to place a tag with your business address without company name on your bags. In the event you are claiming a lost bag, your picture ID with proof of business address will suffice.

• Bring and utilize luggage ties to secure luggage and ensure the safety of your belongings while they are left unattended in a hotel room

• It is recommended to not register or make reservations in one's own name if the individual is well known and prone to attracting unwanted attention

• When possible, book hotel rooms between the second and seventh floors to limit first floor access while still being positioned safely for emergency evacuation if necessary

Travel Precautions

• Always maintain a low profile

• Avoid routine patterns and vary travel routes

• Be conscious of being followed

• Never leave a laptop unattended and only travel with needed data by utilizing removable media/data storage

• Affix an identification label to the outside of laptop to avoid confusion of ownership while processing through secure checkpoints

• Morning arrivals and departures are recommended

• Take caution when conversing with strangers despite their personal appearance

- Avoid traveling with items that are not absolutely necessary

- Limit items to be carried

- Dine in recognized eateries not off the beaten path

- Avoid street vendor food

- While flying, remain at the entrance of the metal detector until your bags have gone through the X-ray machine and never let them out of your sight for any time period

- If flying commercially, once on the plane, keep your carry on beneath your seat in lieu of in the overhead compartment

- While traveling by train, enter and remain in only those cars that are occupied

- Do not joke about weapons and/or explosives

Personal Safety Upon Arrival

From airport arrival, travel to the hotel and throughout your stay, there is a great deal that can be done to enhance overall personal safety. At each and every destination, providing the previously mentioned front-end precautions were taken, the following should be practiced as the rule, not the exception.

- Keep door locked while in the room

- Avoid public areas of the hotel as criminal/terrorist activity is drawn to these areas

- Do not, under any circumstances, discuss the nature of the trip with anyone and be cautious of the information discussed over the telephone

• Avoid nighttime activity away from the hotel if feasible

• If away from hotel, always watch drinks while they are being poured and never leave them unattended

• Be sure any time a credit card is used it is promptly returned and do not give it to bartender to establish a tab

• Avoid using your own name when making social reservations

• Ensure that daily contact is made with the delegated point of contact (POC) and that contingencies are developed

Assessing International Travel Risk

Conduct due diligence on the location(s) of travel to determine an accurate threat based upon the following checklist:

• Social issues

• General crime and corruption issues (to include limits to personal rights if held by local authorities)

• Active terrorist groups

• Organized crime activity

• Propensity for kidnap and extortion

• Labor instability

• Local ethnic/extremist religious issues

• Infrastructure and environmental situation

• Political climate

- Economic strength and income discrepancy

- Health and public safety risks

- Areas not to visit, roads not to travel, taxis not to take and rentals not to use

- Weather concerns

- Hotels/restaurants/hospitals/clinics not to frequent

- Secure travel contingencies in the event of a disruption in schedule

The advisor should recommend a reliable personal protection specialist and security driver (24/7) once the travel due diligence is completed and it is determined the intended destination presents substantial risks. Once it is determined the threat level has been addressed, the following preparations and precautions should be taken:

- Obtain foreign currency in advance, consisting of small denominations, and avoid carrying large sums of cash

- Program cellular phones with local one-touch emergency telephone numbers

- Identify medical facilities in and around the area(s) of destination in advance

- Bring a copy of passport, driver's license and related visa documents to be kept in a separate location in the event of being lost or stolen

- Leave your passports in the hotel safe (providing it is a well-known, internationally recognized property)

- Carry a card with personal medical information, including blood type, medications (including those causing allergic reactions) and physician contact numbers

• Only use ATMs during the day and preferably inside a bank

• Beware of pickpockets and the common techniques they use (distractions, such as jostling, spilling something on you, asking for directions or the time, solicitation of items, and small groups, oftentimes of children, that you must pass through)

• Ensure daily communications are scheduled in advance with point of contact (POC)

• Develop consistent code words/phrases to alert POC to an adverse situation

CHAPTER
8

Identity Theft

Protecting Family Information

Privacy, confidentiality and trusted anonymity are the baseline expectations of the affluent individual and the responsibility of the advisor to ensure their adherence. With the variety of mediums information is disseminated through today, ensuring the client's interests are constantly protected must be at the forefront of every advisor. We remember sitting in a client's conference room (a CPA firm) listening to two gentlemen describe the in-depth security strategy they incorporated to protect their client's information, and, when they were finished, we asked them how long the client files (with all their tax information) had been left out on the table in the conference room for copying. They had no response and changed the subject (now that left us feeling confident). This is a prime example of how information gets stolen because it is left unattended during business hours while visitors roam unescorted and after business hours when cleaning crews (whom you don't know and have had limited if any background done on them) have unfettered access to your office. For the record, this is not uncommon and certainly is not limited to accountants, as we have seen this in law firms, private banks and family offices as well. Moreover, it should be duly noted that once your identity is stolen, it is gone forever. All the advertised services in the world offering post incident assistance will not erase the future risk!

Non Disclosure Agreement (NDA)

At the onset of the relationship, advisors should consider providing each affluent client with a written NDA, illustrating the following:

• Definition of confidential information

• Internal controls of safeguarding information

• Assurance of not duplicating and/or repeating shared information

• Assurance that clients will not be used for marketing purposes

From The RCS Files – Flash Drive Blunder
During the hectic time of tax season, the family was unavailable to meet with their accountant at his office. To ensure compliance of quickly approaching filing deadlines, the family CPA decided to mail a USB flash drive with all family tax information to the client for review. No precautions were taken to use an encrypted device or to protect the data, which made the information available to anyone who inserted the device into a computer. The family received the package with a note from the post office stating the package was inadvertently torn open, and no contents were enclosed.

RCS was engaged to conduct an investigation in attempts to recover the flash drive and assess what damage was done to the family and if their identity had been compromised.

The fact the CPA firm decided to send it through the U.S. Postal Service, even though registered, did not utilize a delivery service, failed to use an encrypted devise and did not password-protect the data exposed them to extensive legal exposure. The eventual financial settlement received by the family did not resolve the fact that their personal information has been compromised or relieve the anguish and feeling of betrayal experienced by them.

Safeguarding Your Social Security Number

The FBI considers identity theft the fastest growing crime in the U.S., and the trend is continuing. Organized crime is actively pursuing this area since the return is high and making prosecutable cases is difficult. When it comes to protecting your personal information and identity, you are only as safe as your weakest link. The challenges that we all face is that our information is everywhere, even if we use secure websites, have encrypted passwords and shred all of our documents. What level of security does everyone else have who has possession of our information? Look at all the doctor offices that have obtained your social security number (SSN), requested a copy of your driver's license and your date of birth. How about the 17-year-old file clerk who is then responsible for filing that information? Remember, you have no obligation to provide your SSN to health care providers (unless you are requesting federal assistance) or other organizations unless required by law. It becomes obvious you can be doing everything right but have no control over what others who have your information are doing.

The following organizations can require your SSN:

- IRS

- Employers

- Accountant

- Creditors

• Mortgage lenders

• Financial service providers

If your wallet is lost or stolen, you can replace the contents, such as credit cards and debit cards, but don't tell us you also carry your social security card. What happens when non-changing information like your social security number is obtained by identity thieves? The fact is, once it is in their hands, it is gone. Identity thieves buy, trade and sell stolen information and use it repeatedly for many years.

At the forefront of most affluent client's list of concerns is protecting their identity. However, the point that advisors must make clear to their clients is that there are no assurances that their identity won't be stolen or that it has not already been compromised. Preemptive measures are vital to reduce the likelihood of this horrific crime occurring; however, equally important is to have deployed appropriate monitoring measures to quickly identify if, in fact, their identity has been compromised. The basic measures the advisor should counsel their clients on are as follows:

Avoidance Measures

• All personal checks should display name and address other than personal residence

• All charitable donations should be made under the name of the company/fund in lieu of the family name to avoid unnecessary exposure

• All documents containing personal information such as social security number, date of birth, address, medical insurance information, credit card numbers and PINs should be shredded with confetti-cut shredders prior to discarding

• If personal information is stored electronically, ensure it is properly encrypted

• Avoid mail delivery to your personal residence

• Internet purchases should only be done with one specific credit card for this purpose only and that card should have a very low credit limit

• Use unique passwords and PINs on all accounts, avoiding mother's maiden name, spouse's name, anniversary/birth dates and children's names

• Examine your credit report once per quarter to ensure no unauthorized activity has occurred (more frequently if a problem is detected)

• Ensure that all doctor's offices utilized have implemented and enforce Health Insurance Portability and Accountability Act (HIPAA) procedures

• If utilizing a travel agency, ensure best practice security measures are in place to protect all your personal information and travel itinerary

Popular Scams to Steal Your Identity

As long as there are people on earth, some will always look for ways to prey on the innocent and unsuspecting. There are long histories of con men and women who are always trying ways to perpetrate the latest scam to enrich themselves through the misfortune of others. It is important to become familiar with the latest scams and be able to quickly identify new variations so as not to become a victim. Verify the legitimacy of any request or offer. Remember, if it sounds too good to be true, it is. Once you independently authenticate the request, limit the amount of sensitive information you provide. There should be no reason to ever give a PIN, password or social security number over the phone to anyone.

Probably one of the most publicized ongoing solicitations is known as the Nigerian email money transfer scam. These emails are sent to thousands of email addresses claiming they have millions of dollars that needs to be moved into a U.S.-based bank for a variety of reasons. They offer a large percentage of the money to anyone willing to help. All that is required is for you to furnish your banking information so money can be transferred into your account. Once this is completed, you simply send the money to another bank, not yet identified, minus the percentage for your assistance. Sounds simple, right? The problem is once they have knowledge of your banking information and with their ability to exploit technology within the banking system, they will actually remove the proceeds from your account. This also allows them to take this information and, unbeknownst to you, open up other unauthorized accounts and obtain credit in your name.

There have been numerous government task force investigations assigned to this project; however, the scam continues, and individuals still fall prey to these con artists. These individuals tend to be sincere and oftentimes appear to be victims themselves, which creates sympathy of unsuspecting honest individuals who want to "help." In the past year, we have been approached by two victims who both lost significant amounts of money through this scam.

Another well-known scam is perpetrated through online auctions such as eBay. After a potential victim sells an item, the buyer asks them to accept a cashier's check for payment. The buyer then sends a check for a greater amount than the purchase. He follows up with a convincing call stating his secretary made a mistake and switched checks. He asks if the seller will deposit the cashier's check and send a check for the difference along with the merchandise. This is done; however, about a week after the cashier's check was deposited, it is determined to be fraudulent. Never deposit any type of check on someone's behalf and give them proceeds until your bank has confirmed its authenticity and the funds are in your account.

There are many of you saying that you would never fall prey to these or the even more complex scams that are popular today. However, sophisticated scam artists are becoming increasingly more effective in tricking a broader segment of the population.

There is increasing popularity with bank account scams since that's where the money is. An individual claiming to be a financial services representative informs you there is a problem with your account or you are the victim of identity theft. The criminal usually has some of your personal information that they easily obtained from the Internet. They will then convince you to provide additional personal information that needs to be "verified" so they can resolve the issue.

Have you ever received an email from your bank requesting you to follow the attached link and log on to your account? As scam artists become more creative, so do their phishing email messages and pop-up windows. They often include official looking logos from legitimate organizations and other identifying information taken directly from their websites. They send messages such as "If you don't respond within 48 hours, your account will be closed." These messages convey a sense of urgency so that you will respond immediately and follow the directions outlined. Phishing emails might also claim that your response is required because your account may have been compromised. These messages are usually sent out in bulk so they often are addressed as "Dear Valued Customer" and do not contain your first or last name. These messages will unwittingly draw you to legitimate-looking websites, which are actually the phony scam sites (otherwise referred to as "man in the middle attacks"), where they attempt to have you provide personal log-on information.

The victims of this wave of recent phishing activity were clients of two of the country's largest banking institutions. Investigation by the FBI resulted in the arrest and identification of over 100 individuals who were complicit in phishing email activities responsible for deceiving bank customers of millions of dollars. In the traditional way of phishing, email received seems legitimate and comes from the counterfeit sites in question and offers a link to a fraudulent website mimicking that of the financial institution. From this page, the user was prompted to enter their personal and financial information. The stolen money was paid into the bank accounts of criminals based in the United States then transferred to associates in other countries.

Another scam impacting us all is the jury duty scam. You receive an official-looking notice advising you have missed your scheduled jury duty date. Once you call the listed number and state you never received the summons, you are asked to verify your name and address, which the caller provides to you. He then explains the serious consequences of not appearing for jury duty and the potential criminal ramifications. To ensure there has been no bench warrant issued, he requests your SSN and date of birth to access the system so you do not have any additional problems. Once he has this information, your problems have just begun.

It is important to protect yourself from these and many other scams that are going around. Take the time to verify the legitimacy and identity of anyone prior to furnishing sensitive information. Do not succumb to compelling reasons to provide personal information and adhere to the following recommendations:

- Independently verify the legitimacy of all calls or correspondence prior to opening dialogue

- Do not verify any information someone already has about you

- Do not cash a check or transfer money for anyone who is a mere acquaintance

- Never provide SSN online or over the phone

- Never log into any of your online accounts from a link you received in an email

- Do not believe anyone can get you a new SSN account number

- Place a fraud alert or extended fraud alert on your credit report

- Provide updated contact information to all credit bureaus

- Review credit reports from all reporting agencies annually

- If you suspect fraud, notify organizations possibly affected, close accounts, and change passwords and PINs

Hotel Key Cards

Do you know what is on the majority of those magnetic key cards provided at luxury hotels?

- Your name

- Partial home address

- Hotel room number

- Dates of stay

- Credit card number and expiration date

- Gambling activity (in hotels where legal gaming is available)

If, at conclusion of your stay, key cards are returned to the front desk, left in your room or disposed in the trash, your personal information is available to be accessed through a card-scanning device. Once this is done, the information can be downloaded onto a computer and your identity compromised.

To avoid the possibility of identity theft, you can pass a magnet across the magnetic strip several times which will erase all information on the card.

CHAPTER
9

TECHNICAL SURVEILLANCE COUNTERMEASURES (TSCM)

From The RCS Files – Smile, You're On Hidden Camera
During a Technical Surveillance Countermeasures (TSCM) inspection, an RCS specialist was using a thermal imager to identify heat anomalies within a private residence infrequently used by the owner. While viewing the bedroom area, a hot spot was detected in a built in bookshelf. Upon closer inspection, behind several books was a covert video camera that was transmitting wirelessly to the Internet for illegal remote viewing. After consulting with the client, RCS removed the device, assisted with damage control and facilitated the subsequent law enforcement investigation. It should be noted that this type of crime is being perpetrated against a vast array of the affluent community without regard to celebrity status. The focus being on the

potential revenue stream that can be obtained through blackmail by these nefarious types of individuals.

A comprehensive TSCM inspection, commonly referred to as a sweep, includes the electronic analysis and physical inspection of specific locations to detect and identify interceptions of private conversations, covert video or other vulnerabilities. The process requires a variety of specialized equipment to ensure comprehensive inspection of the area in question to include all communications systems.

Equipment must be able to provide the following:

- Spectrum analysis to identify burst transmissions and frequency hopping

- Digital telephone analysis to identify phone taps

- Testing of all electrical, computer and communication lines for intercept devices

- Use of thermal imagery to view suspect heat signatures

- X-ray of suspicious areas

- Physical inspection to detect hidden electronic devices

Information is the lifeblood for most enterprises today. Technological advances, while making communication easier and instantaneous, has a major downside when it comes to protecting personal and proprietary information. The reasons to conduct a TSCM are varied; however, they are generally classified as preventive, reactive or a combination of both. The appropriate time to conduct a TSCM is dependent on the following considerations:

- You need to be assured the utmost privacy for your activities or discussions

- You are preparing to conduct strategic planning meetings, enter into contract negotiations, discuss proprietary information or send confidential data transmissions, and you need confirmation the location is secure from unauthorized intercepts

• You have suspicions that proprietary information has been compromised, causing concern that an eavesdropping device has been installed at the location where confidential meetings were held.

• You are preparing to move into a recently remodeled or newly purchased residence.

With the miniaturization of computer storage, intercept devices will also continue to become smaller, less costly and less easily detected. Each week, 150–200 eavesdropping devices are sold on eBay. The variety of items offered are limitless, from telephones, fax machines and computers to a variety of common office items that have been converted into intercept devices such as proximity card readers. Some are manufactured overseas and placed on operating frequencies that ensure optimal transition ranges with little chance of discovery or interference. Most of these devices are priced under $100 and can be used with inexpensive scanners or called up with your own telephone to monitor the intercept.

It is imperative to know that your information, conversations and actions are secure from prying eyes and ears to protect against crimes such as extortion, espionage and theft. Any area where there is an expectation of privacy, such as offices, boardrooms, homes, vehicles, planes or yachts, are prime targets for unauthorized eavesdropping.

TSCM Methodology

The following equipment and expertise are the benchmark in the industry for a comprehensive TSCM inspection. You must be cautious of firms in the marketplace without this requisite level of sophisticated equipment. To ensure devices and transmissions can be identified and traced to their origin requires cutting-edge technology, without which the inspection is not truly comprehensive.

Equally important is the level of expertise of the individuals conducting the TSCM inspection. They must have the training and experience to differentiate between routine signals and various anomalies. Ideally, you should identify individuals formerly from the government intelligence community who have experience doing court-authorized covert installations. Individuals with this expertise will be aware of the latest technology, installation requirements and likely locations of covert devices.

Remember, each step eliminated in the process outlined below can be the unexplored area where a device can go undetected.

• A threat evaluation is made and discussed with the client

• Digital telephone system analysis, including instruments, incoming trunks, in-house cabling and peripheral equipment, for intercept devices

• A radio frequency (RF) spectrum analysis from 10 KHz to 21 GHz that includes recognition capabilities for standard analog devices in addition to digital, spread-spectrum and the previously not available capability of detecting frequency-hopping transmitters

• An infrared (IR) search of all appropriate access areas to detect and locate intercept systems using optics to relay communications (IR, laser, etc.)

• Electronic inspections for covert video transmissions

• A carrier current RF spectrum analysis of AC outlets, telephone cable, computer lines and other wiring, as appropriate, to detect devices capable of transmitting communications

• An electronic search of the area with a nonlinear junction detector to detect and locate dormant (on or off) or remotely activated communication and recording devices

• An optic search of the area with a thermal imager to detect and locate communication and recording devices providing heat signatures

• Use of portable X-ray system to eliminate false positives from other tests and to view inside walls and other inaccessible areas Acoustic leakage testing with amplifiers and contact microphones to determine loss of communications through air ducts, water pipes, windows, etc.

• Analysis of all wire runs either into or out of the concerned area A physical search of the target site for hidden microphones, transmitters, audio recorders, closed-circuit television (CCTV) systems and any other interception devices

• An on-site oral report followed by detailed written analysis depicting survey equipment, methodology, observations and recommendations

What Is an Intercept Device?

Traditional intercept devices are secreted in large objects or installed in remote areas that are not easily accessible. For instance, a standalone device that can easily fit inside a telephone interface device is designed to monitor conversations inside the home. Entry inside the residence is not required, just access to the telephone box typically on the exterior of the residence. Installation can be accomplished in as little as 60 seconds. The device uses the voltage of the telephone line for power and transmits all residential phone calls to a nearby monitoring location, often inside a vehicle. There are certain technologies that can avoid this from happening; however, the simplest is to ensure your telephone box is secured.

We have experienced major advances in telephone systems used in the workplace. One of these advancements is the conference telephone often found in boardrooms, conference rooms and offices. Over the years, there have been updates to make these instruments more secure; however, they can still be compromised. The primary manufacturer of these devices is Polycom. The most common Polycom is an analog telephone susceptible to covert interception of telephone or room conversation. This instrument passes speech to the existing telephone PBX over copper cabling within the building. Quite often, companies have updated their telephone system to a fully digital system; however, they still provide capability for analog phone lines for fax machines, emergency disaster phones, etc., through the digital switch/PBX. This analog voice path remains vulnerable wherever the cabling is accessible.

Today, devices come in all shapes and sizes. They are becoming increasingly easier to obtain and no longer available to just law enforcement and government agencies. Advances in technology have resulted in the miniaturization of eavesdropping devices that don't look out of place in any environment. Further, they still have the capability to perform as designed and have storage capacities far beyond what was available just several years ago. These types of inconspicuous recording devices, both audio and video, are appearing throughout the corporate and private world.

There is a working ballpoint pen that also houses a covert camera, microphone and digital recorder. The recorder is activated by depressing the single button on the top of the pen. This records high-resolution color video and crystal clear audio on the internal 4 GB storage. To view and or save the captured recording, simply plug the pen into a USB port on your computer. The 4 GB allows for up to 15 hours of recording both video and audio.

There are laser listening devices that have directional light eavesdropping capabilities similar to systems that have been available and used by governments and law enforcement for many years. These older systems were very manpower intensive and required a listening post close to the target of the intercept. While technological advances continue to bring new products to the market, a single package laser system was developed that is available in spy shops. The laser is approximately the size of a VCR. It houses both transmit and receive optic systems, unlike systems of the past. The laser beam is reflected off the target window where it intercepts vibrations caused by conversations inside the room. These window vibrations are converted to useable audio by the receive optics and electronic package.

The miniaturization of covert intercept devices continues to be developed. A USB flash drive also serves as a voice recorder and discreetly records up to 40 hours of audio. It looks just like a USB drive so no one will know you are recording. After recording the conversation, simply plug the USB device into any computer and upload and email your recordings. Playback is with Windows Media Player.

From The RCS Files – Are You Listening?
While an RCS technician was performing a visual inspection of various electronic instruments, cabling, wall jacks and fax machine located in the client's home office, he observed a device connected to the remote modular plug on the fax machine. Upon closer inspection, he observed what appeared to be a microphone within the epoxy material. To determine the device capabilities, a telephone call was placed to the fax machine. After the first ring, room conversation could be heard over the handset once a call was placed to the fax machine. The first call was terminated and a second call was placed. On this second attempt to monitor conversations, the fax machine answered and provided the signaling handshake for two communicating fax machines. A couple of further tests were performed, and it was determined that the intercept device allowed faxes to be received 50 percent of the time, while outgoing faxes could be sent 100 percent of the time.

A Trap-Trace was initiated through the local phone company, and further investigation identified the caller as a competitor of our client. The client advised that this individual had been in his residence on several occasions. It was obvious that this device was placed on the fax machine to monitor room conversations from remote locations. This case was handed to the local prosecutor for criminal filing.

In conjunction with the performance of a TSCM inspection, an IT audit is recommended. Access to confidential or proprietary information is equally likely to be found on a computer as it is during a TSCM inspection. To ensure complete peace of mind, both are necessary precautions. It was during the course of a TSCM inspection that a technician, performing the radio frequency (RF) analysis, detected a UHF signal of concern. The RF signal was isolated to an office where it appeared that the transmission of room conversations was emanating from a desktop printer. Further inspection disclosed that a small UHF transmitter was housed inside a USB printer cable. The transmitter was secreted inside what appeared to be a standard interference coil. With this device in place, conversations could easily be monitored from outside the facility. If an IT audit were not being conducted in conjunction with the TSCM, the computer and printer would, in all likelihood, not have been powered on, and the device would have been overlooked, since the transmitter was operational only when the equipment was turned on.

Another addition to the eavesdropper's arsenal is a computer key logger that transmits your computer key stokes to a Bluetooth device. The eavesdropper merely needs a cellular phone or a laptop computer with Bluetooth capabilities. Once the key logger is installed inside your keyboard, all key strokes will be transmitted to the intercepting person's device within 300 feet of your area. This device is invisible to the victim, is not affected by firewalls, uses no resources, won't affect software on the target computer, and can't be disabled or detected by security software. Now they don't even need to return to your computer to retrieve the information being entered.

Information Theft's Collateral Risk

When consulting with the affluent client regarding the protection of their information, the advisor must first ensure that his or her own internal procedures meet best practices as they relate to document security, information security and access control procedures. Additionally, providers such as those listed below should be evaluated to ensure compliance:

- Family office

- Law firm

• Accounting firm

• Financial advisor

• Trading floors

• Doctor's office

• Learning institutions

• Social clubs

CHAPTER
10

CLOSE PERSONAL PROTECTION

From The RCS Files – Now That Was Embarrassing
The principal had two full-time bodyguards assigned to him at all times while away from his residence. He left the gate of his gated home open when he departed his residence in the morning, parked his vehicle in a reserved spot identifying him by name and ate regularly two days a week at a neighboring restaurant. Never was a comment received from his bodyguards regarding this pattern of activity. One day while dining at his usual location, with both of the bodyguards sitting at his table, he was surprised by a female who put a pie on his head as she passed his table. The bodyguards immediately jumped up, and, while one threw her to the ground, injuring her back, the other pulled his weapon and held her at gun point.

It was determined the woman was a former girlfriend intent on embarrassing the principal in public. The woman ended up requiring medical treatment and eventually sued over the entire fiasco. There was an undisclosed settlement rumored to be in seven figures. Additionally, it was determined one of the bodyguards had no authority to carry a weapon and was arrested by law enforcement when they arrived on-scene. Several days later, the principal contacted RCS and relayed the aforementioned story. "How can I have been so unlucky?" was one of the quotes he uttered. Lack of luck had nothing to do with his plight. Unfortunately, he had never been schooled in what professional executive protection entails and learned the hard way that large, untrained men are not the panacea for personal security.

In a global world where kidnapping and extortion have become a thriving business, and violence an acceptable vehicle in sending political, religious and personal messages, executive protection of high-profile individuals is no longer a luxury but a necessity. With the unlimited availability of personal and corporate information on the Internet, individuals who were previously under the radar are now easily accessible by criminals and stalkers. Whether a corporate executive, entertainer, athlete or celebrity, you are at an increased risk and an inviting target if the necessary precautions are not implemented. The goal of each assignment should be to provide discrete port-to-port protection through a cadre of proven professionals. This is accomplished through tenacious preparation, effective risk management and realistic contingency planning to ensure appropriate security measures are in place to mitigate critical vulnerabilities.

The approach to executive protection needs to be strategically focused on four major tenets: preparation, education, communication and coordination, which are delivered in the following manner:

- Personal risk assessment conducted on client and family

- Vulnerability assessments conducted at all locations that client frequents

- Comprehensive and ongoing intelligence gathering

- Identified roles and responsibilities of client and protection professionals

• Established operational and communications security

• Post-trip debriefing for continued efficiency of service

A variety of individuals believe they need to employ bodyguards to accompany them when traveling, attending public events or when they feel their safety is in jeopardy. Usually this entails engaging an individual who is large in stature who stays close by the principal to keep others away. This individual is the last line of defense and is quick to be identified by their size, proximity to principal, clothing and aggressive actions. To the untrained eye, it appears that the bodyguard is providing close personal protection and will be able to quickly address attacks if they should occur.

Although dealing with an individual of large physical stature can be challenging, this is relying on the fact that the bodyguard can defeat single or multiple attackers, not be distracted by a diversion and still monitor and/or evacuate the principal. The attacker has the advantage by having already identified his adversary prior to the bodyguard recognizing that an attack is imminent.

A personal protection professional (PPP) will rely on his or her ability to assess the situation and the crowd from more of a distance. They do not want to attract undue attention, so they blend in with the principal. They dress in a like manner, are similar in demeanor, are oftentimes the same sex and are well-trained. They follow a pre-deployment checklist to ensure they have prepared as thoroughly as possible prior to deployment, which allows them to be proactive rather than reactive. They rely on their ability to continually assess the situation from a short distance, allowing them to anticipate an attack prior to it occurring, rather than reacting to an attack once it has occurred.

When to Utilize Personal Protection Professionals?

A PPP is utilized by the principal for one of the following reasons:

- Known threat – high threat

- Perceived threat – low threat

- Desire for protection based on position or stature – escort

Contrary to what many believe, it is easier to protect an individual who has known threats against them rather than other scenarios when the threat is unknown. Once a threat has already been made, investigation can be conducted to identify the individual making the threat, allowing intelligence and background information to be obtained.

The following intelligence packet should be compiled on the individual making the threat:

- Photograph of subject

- Current physical description

- Current whereabouts

- Activities, skills and abilities

- Background investigation identifying criminal history

- Current residence

- Vehicles owned and operated

- Evaluation of type of threat

- Determine likelihood of executing threat

With this information at hand, the PPP is now in a position to properly address the threat and ensure the safety of the principal.

When a threat is merely perceived, it is oftentimes more difficult to defend than when dealing with a direct threat. For instance, you receive a note on the front seat of your car saying your daughter is in danger of being kidnapped. You don't know if this was just a random crank note, a "practical joke" by someone who knows where you park, an attempt to preoccupy you by taking your attention off of other important activities or an actual warning from a co-conspirator who doesn't want to see this occur. It does not originate from a direct source that can be investigated, and you are not sure if the threat is even legitimate. Obviously, when continued warnings occur, you begin to take the threat more seriously. However, you still need to ensure appropriate precautions are taking place in the event the threat is legitimate.

An individual's notoriety, media exposure or affluence may require a PPP to provide added peace of mind. It is important the role of the PPP is clearly defined and they do not take on the role of carrying shopping bags, running errands, parking cars or pushing baby strollers. Their role is to provide for the security and safety of the principal and not the role of personal assistant. All too often, when there is not a known threat, the PPP is drawn into roles that are not in the principal's best interest. Just because there are not any known threats does not eliminate the potential for an attack to occur.

Pre-deployment Check List

Once the determination has been made that executive protection is required, the assigned PPPs conduct a variety of activities outlined in the pre-deployment checklist:

• Review threat assessment on principal

• Evaluate travel locations and conduct advance work, if feasible

- Analyze any known threats and employ sufficient counter-measures

- Articulate rules of engagement and emergency protocols

- Ensure updated medical plan

When conducting the threat assessment on the principal, all prior threats must be considered. You need to evaluate any potential threats and the reason they have engaged a PPP. Identify who is traveling, the location and duration of travel, activities at the location, purpose of travel and if accommodations are required once you arrive. Special evaluation needs to be conducted if travel is for an extended period or is to be outside the United States. Determine if the principal is flying commercially or by private aircraft and what the ground transportation arrangements are prior to departure and upon arrival. Once these determinations are made, you can decide if doing advance work is feasible, which is usually determined by the level of risk facing the principal. Once the threat assessment is completed and all modes of travel identified, the PPP will evaluate the points of greatest vulnerability and make arrangements to harden those areas thus minimizing the risk to the principal.

If the principal is taking a trip, the selection of personnel is critical based upon the results of the threat assessment. Identifying the number of individuals in the detail, or the need for a female, a language-speaker or other special skills based on the activities of the principal must all be decided. For instance, if the principal is going to Colorado for a ski trip, having PPPs who are experienced skiers is a must. Once the team is identified, scheduling is done to ensure adequate coverage will be on hand to cover the trip.

Rules of engagement must be discussed and agreed upon by the principal prior to assignment. This will determine the requirements and parameters placed on the PPP during the assignment. For instance, the principal may not want the PPP inside his residence and request he wait in the vehicle while at the residence. He may require someone who is close by at all times, which, to do properly, will require a second individual to observe and assess the situation, since the other person will be too close to foresee a situation prior to developing. The principal may be more concerned of unflattering pictures being taken or other situations that will not cause physical harm to the principal but will cause embarrassment. It is important to fully understand the principal's concerns and desires prior to initiating the assignment as well as for the principal to understand the expectations of his protection team so as to eliminate ambiguity which can lead to adverse scenarios.

A major component of all security assignments is to understand any medical conditions impacting the principal. For instance, if the principal is a diabetic, the PPP needs to know where the principal carries insulin and how to administer in the event there is a diabetic attack. All medical conditions, including allergies, are important information for the PPP to obtain in advance so certain situations can be avoided that may further put the principal's health in jeopardy. In addition, the PPP should, at all times, know the location of the closest hospital and have the ability to summon medical professionals if required.

Protecting the Children

Oftentimes, the PPP is engaged solely to look after the principal's children. Due to the status and notoriety of the principal, the family may have become unsuspecting targets as a way to retaliate against the principal or receive a quick payday by extortion or blackmail. The PPP assigned to protect family members does not take on the role of nanny or new best friend. They work closely with other caregivers but remain at arm's length from the protectee in terms of getting emotionally involved or "too close" to maintain a professional demeanor. They need to remain vigilant to potential danger, and this cannot be accomplished if they have taken on the role of companion or playmate.

Confidential Personal Profile Record

Information should be obtained from each protectee prior to initiating any long-term assignments. This is even a higher priority when travelling overseas. Once the form is completed, it should be discussed with the security team leader and then sealed in an envelope by the individual and maintained in a safe location. It is imperative that the report is amended whenever any significant changes occur.

Refer to Confidential Personal Profile in Appendix A.

Code word information can be used in several different ways if the victim has been schooled in how to respond to questions. In each of the profile sections of the portfolio, certain words should be highlighted. These words indicate subject matter that only a victim or their family would know. For example, if someone indicated they had kidnapped the family patriarch and was holding him for ransom, but no family member was able to verify this was true, a question could be asked of the kidnappers, "How old was the victim when he lost the tip of his finger?" If the subjects would not allow the victim to speak directly, then they would have to ask him to provide the correct answer. This would indicate several things: It would verify he was taken hostage and that he is still alive. But if they cannot answer these questions, it is a good indication that they do not have a hostage or they are unable to communicate with the victim.

Another consideration in the use of code words is to train the person to make cryptic statements that provide others an understanding of the situation. Words that indicate they are being held hostage, if there are others, if they are injured, if they are close by or if their life is in immediate peril would all be relevant information for the crisis response team. These words would be set forth in this section with an explanation as to how they would be used in a conversation and their intended meaning.

Armed vs. Unarmed

The question continually asked is whether having armed or unarmed protection is best. Most often, individuals immediately think having someone with a weapon is preferred. If you were to research the number of times that professional protection details actually pull their weapons, you would realize it is a remarkably small number of times, and there are even fewer occasions when weapons are actually discharged. The reason for the low occurrence of weapons use is based upon the extensive amount of training and experience of the detail, coupled with the appropriate advance work. The greater skill is for the PPP to have thorough training in conflict avoidance so they are able to foresee dangerous situations and avoid confrontations. The PPP should have knowledge of weaponless defense techniques, but the primary role of the PPP is to evacuate the principal from danger, not to confront it. What is key to remember is that a firearm is presented only to exercise deadly physical force not to be a showpiece.

Another concern with regard to weapon use is ensuring there is sufficient authority to do so. If a PPP pulls a weapon to move back a crowd, he is doing so in a threatening manner, not in response to an imminent threat. The exposure to a lawsuit being filed, which could ultimately impact the principal, increases exponentially when a weapon comes into play. Recently, we have seen many lawsuits when weapons were accidently discharged, left unattended or taken away and used on the individual initially displaying the weapon.

There may be situations, based on the threat assessment, that having armed security with concealed weapons is warranted. It is important to ensure that weapons are legally being carried and those individuals carrying meet state and federal requirements. With the passage of HR 218, The Law Enforcement Officer Safety Act, this eases the requirements for current or former qualified law enforcement officers, allowing them to carry a concealed firearm across state lines. For individuals who are not HR 218 qualified, having a concealed weapon permit requires special training and licensing and is not necessarily reciprocal with other states, and will not be allowed in other countries. If an assignment requires armed security, be sure that the following criteria are strictly adhered to:

• Validate background and training of individual armed

• Validate a concealed weapons permit (CCW) for the state in which it will be carried

- Review qualification requirements for weapon(s) carried on continual basis

- Ensure compliance if qualifying under HR 218 (Law Enforcement Officer Safety Act)

- Ensure sufficient insurance requirements are maintained by individual(s) carrying weapons

Stalkers

Principals frequently request the assistance of security when they are the victim of a stalker. A stalker is typically a known threat, so a great amount of advance work can be done to identify this individual and study their habits prior to deployment. Stalkers cannot be taken lightly and their history of long-term annoyance and violence is well documented. It is imperative a thorough understanding of the stalker's objectives are understood, since there are distinct differences of how you would deal with a stalker who has an imaginary love interest and someone who wants to discredit or harm the principal.

Estate Security

There may be situations, based on the threat assessment, that having armed security at the principal's residence on a 24/7 basis is warranted. Estate security is designed to augment the PPP by ensuring the estate grounds are free of intruders at all times. Estate security personnel need to remain outside the residence where they can conduct unscheduled patrols and be alert to unusual sounds or activity. Their presence can be augmented by having a viewing station of the perimeter camera surveillance system. In the event there is a breach at the estate, they can immediately notify the PPP inside the residence who will advise the principal, giving sufficient time to enter a designated safe area.

Deploying armed security on your estate, although costly, will deter intruders and help protect the family if there is an intrusion attempt.

Chapter 11

MITIGATING YOUR
WORST NIGHTMARE

Bad Things Happen to Good People

Every 28 seconds, an aggravated assault is committed. Every five minutes, a woman is raped. Each year, nearly two of every three new businesses fail. And nearly 60 percent of all marriages end in divorce, leaving tens of thousands of children to be raised by single parents.

This is unfortunate but true—as we witness in the news on a daily basis. No one can prepare themselves for the body-numbing experience felt if a loved one is killed, harmed, missing or abducted. While we try not to live our lives in fear of this occurrence happening, it is something we all carry inside us to some degree. We tell ourselves violence happens without warning and that it happens to other people and not to us. Unfortunately, nothing is further from the truth. People who find themselves a victim of crime seldom anticipated such an event occurring. We all have some degree of ability to predict violence as we have the ability of fight or flight. What is necessary is to appropriately utilize this innate ability while living our everyday lives.

The Impact of a Crisis

The inability to properly react to a crisis situation is often the result of stress caused by the escalation of events. Is our reaction to stress the only cause? Of course not. But it is a major one. Thus, if we can teach ourselves to properly prepare for stressful situations, we minimize the danger of escalating stressful events into major catastrophes. As a result, we will be more successful, and our lives more rewarding and peaceful.

You must learn to condition your mind so that you can replace "panic" with "reason" as your primary course of action in a stressful situation. The key in preparation is to have a plan. If you don't, you need to bring in the right individual or company that can quickly grasp the situation, based upon extensive experience, and develop a plan of action to be followed. You need to know before you step into the "arena" what your options are and how you will react to unexpected situations, no matter how stressful situations may become.

There is a phrase we hear over and over again from victims of crime: "I can't believe it happened to me!" Many highly stressful situations, those that are often life-altering or business-altering, happen fast. No warning. BANG! There it is right in front of you with little time to figure out. How many times have we recently read in the newspaper about a well-known political figure suddenly exposed for some type of sexual encounter? How many can remember their names and the outcome? The one's you don't remember is because they took action to address the situation swiftly to minimize damage and exposure. Those who land back on their feet the quickest are always the ones who developed a plan to include contingencies.

How you react in that stressful moment of truth is the difference between success and failure, perhaps even life and death. The goal, therefore, is to plan for crisis situations. If we plan for unexpected contingencies, then they no longer take the form of truly unexpected matters. By way of example, antiterrorist units in the FBI continually train for worst-case scenarios when doing high-risk protection details or room entries so they can anticipate the behavior of hostile individuals lying in wait. Conceptually, it is this form of "training" strategy that is applicable to most aspects of a crisis.

When we train and condition our minds to react in a certain way, that is how we will react when under pressure. Consider the security driver responsible for driving the female executive to and from her office. All goes according to plan, and there is no stress. Now imagine the scenario where a vehicle tries to cut off the driver and abduct the executive. This is not the time for the driver to just freeze and await the consequences.

Conversely, an experienced veteran, having prepared for this and similar scenarios, reacts to the stress by doing what he was trained to do: continue to accelerate and deploy proven defensive maneuvers to avoid capture. The notion of accelerating the vehicle is an example of conditioning a reaction to a crisis. The inexperienced security driver, who is not so trained, will panic and slow the vehicle, allowing the abductors the opportunity to accomplish their goal.

The first step toward reconditioning the mind is to redefine notions of stress. In the context of everyday life stressors that we all experience, rather than viewing stress as something to avoid, we must view it positively as part of our life. Stress challenges us. It pushes us to new limits and levels of achievement we never thought possible. Stress cannot be thought of as a negative.

Without properly conditioning your mind the woman walking home at night will not be able to react properly to the surprise attack of a mugger. The surgeon will not be able to react properly when his patient goes into cardiac arrest. Parents will not be able to react appropriately when their 16-year-old daughter is abducted. Rather, they all will panic. Prepare for the unexpected so that stress-induced panic is not your automatic first course of action.

But what exactly is stress? Despite numerous attempts to define stress over the years, no satisfactory definition has emerged. But what we do know is that stress often refers to the circumstances responsible for how we behave. And, more often than not, stress is the resultant feeling of fear. That fear can take the shape of fearing the unknown, fear of not knowing what to do, fear of failure, fear of injury, fear of losing money, fear of losing a competition, fear of losing respect, fear of losing a companionship and fear of whatever else you may face.

It follows, therefore, that if we can eliminate or reduce the level of fear, we can reduce the level of stress. After all, we do not tend to panic when good things happen, only when bad things happen, or when we anticipate bad things happening for no reason. Matters that "go as planned" are, by definition, the antithesis of stress. The goal, therefore, is to attempt to identify potential crisis situations that may impact our lives so we can plan for them in the event of an occurrence. Once we identify likely crisis scenarios, then we can prepare for the unexpected.

The key issue is how do we react in a stressful situation? If we can train ourselves so that panic is not the automatic response to stressful situations, then we will be able to transition from everyday common occurrences to a crisis event without panicking. As a result, we will most likely choose the proper course of action that will lead to a successful resolution. In short, by controlling our tendency to panic under stress, we improve greatly our chances for success, no matter what the situation. In sum, we improve the chances of resolving the crisis situation and reducing the overall impact.

In a violent confrontation, what matters most is not how hard you, as the victim, can punch or how perfectly you can execute a self-defense technique. What matters most is how adeptly you can transform your attitude instantaneously from that of a passive victim to that of an active defender. It is that ability to transform your attitude that is the key to conditioning your mind to handle stress in all walks of life, whether in a violent confrontation, a crisis at work or trouble at home.

On the street, panic leads to harm. In business, panic leads to financial ruin. At home, panic leads to broken families.

Is there a way to avoid panic as an automatic response? Yes, and we've seen it over and over around the world in context with elite antiterrorist units, star athletes, renowned doctors, successful attorneys and many others. The secret that they all share is that they have learned how to train their minds so that panic does not become the automatic response to a crisis situation. By properly conditioning your mind, you can eliminate panic as your primary course of action in a stressful situation. The result is that you greatly enhance your chances for success, and diminish the likelihood of escalating the crisis any further. Remember, the key word here is learned behavior so it is incumbent upon you to invest the time to obtain this knowledge and skill.

Crisis Communications

If a public or affluent figure is involved in a crisis situation, extensive media interest will develop once it becomes public. It is important that a proper, well-prepared and consistent message is relayed so no further damage comes to those impacted. Prior identification of a crisis management team that understands the full ramifications of a crisis and can counsel and guide those involved through the process is essential.

Initially there will be a rush to gather as much information about the situation as possible. Let's say a well-known celebrity is the victim of a female stalker. He wants to merely protect his family and self from this individual and retain as much privacy as possible during the ordeal. The stalker, since she is not attracting the required attention of the victim through her stalking efforts, files an erroneous civil suit stating she is the mother of his child. As a result, it becomes public and attracts the media, who now want to delve into every aspect of the athlete's life to try and find the "real story." The following are the type of inquiries the family advisor would need to make in order to prepare for the anticipated onslaught of media attention.

Post-Incident Information

• What is the current situation?

• What has been done so far to control the situation?

• Is there a threat of danger?

• Has the family been secured?

• What security measures have been put in place?

• Have the proper authorities been notified (police, other law enforcement/regulatory authorities) if appropriate?

• Are the media already aware of the incident?

• Are TV crews/reporters on site?

• Have media inquiries been received?

Background Information

• What events led to the incident?

• How long has the stalking been going on?

• How do you know her?

• Has this type of incident previously occurred?

• Is there truth in the allegation?

• What is the estimated financial impact on family, sponsors and career?

Once the information has been collected, it should be inputted into a written format and disseminated to the crisis team members. This will ensure that the entire group is working from the same set of facts. If necessary and appropriate, it should be determined the best manner to convey the information to outside contacts to begin damage control. In all situations, it is essential to verify and double-check all facts that are to going to be released to the public, particularly in cases that are highly sensitive.

Depending on the notoriety of the celebrity or political figure involved the situation may create extensive paparazzi interest. You must be prepared to deal with an onslaught of media interest and to witness the individual being exposed to a plethora of media coverage based on anonymous sources oftentimes having no factual basis or any semblance of the truth. We long ago realized some of the tabloid type media outlets do not let the truth ruin the opportunity to sell a good story. Knowing this in advance you need to be prepared for this onslaught as you prepare the appropriate media strategy to pursue.

Home Invasions

This is one of the most terrifying crimes, and even if unharmed, victims are left mentally scarred, with their lives forever changed. Home invasion is often motivated by a variety of criminal intentions, the most common being robbery. It is a crime that affects you when you are most vulnerable since it occurs in the place where you feel the safest, your home. The following statistics were revealed in a U.S. Department of Justice report:

- 38 percent of assaults and 60 percent of rapes occur during home invasions

- 1 out of every 5 homes will experience a break-in or home invasion

- Statistically, there are over 8,000 home invasions per day in North America

Many victims are commonly observed for hours or days prior to an attack. They may be approached by an individual pretending to be an unassuming or trusted person such as a serviceman, postal carrier, delivery person or neighbor in need of assistance. They use a variety of ruses to get you to open the front door and to invite them into your home. Invasions commonly occur as a result of the homeowner opening the door without first verifying the legitimacy of the visit. In some cases, victims may even receive a pretext phone call informing them that a delivery or a maintenance repairman has been dispatched to their address. Once entry is gained, the attack will be swift, catching the victim totally by surprise during an unsuspecting moment.

On occasion, the attacker will wait until the victim is asleep and violently enter through the front door or a window, terrifying all occupants while immediately looking for cash, jewelry, credit cards and other valuables. Sometimes the invasion is motivated by the desire to procure personal information such as ATM card, PINs, bank account information or tax returns that can later be used for fraudulent purposes.

Among the worst-case scenarios, the criminal's intentions are rape, kidnapping, torture or terror. In these situations, an armed invader takes the victim by surprise and enjoys the power of tormenting powerful and influential individuals who have found themselves helpless in their own homes. It is common for the criminals, or the individual who may have hired them, to have had prior contact with the victims and a specific retaliatory agenda prior to making entry.

A prominent residential community in southern California had over 40 home invasion robberies in a six month period as reported by local police. While these numbers are disturbing, home invasion robberies are not a new phenomenon and are equally as common in other affluent communities throughout the country. Oftentimes, house staff, gardeners and vendors working in exclusive neighborhoods for wealthy families are sometimes the "tipsters" that line up the invasions. They have the ability to be quiet observers without being noticed. Some home invaders might have been in your home before as a delivery person, installer or repair person.

Frequently, the invasions are the work of gangs who mark their victims at exclusive shopping centers or boutiques. The predators watch for potential victims driving luxury vehicles, wearing exclusive clothes and expensive jewelry. Women and elderly people are frequently targeted since they offer little or no resistance when the armed attackers decide to strike. Frequently, the predators will follow the victim home but not attack until they have had time to recon the neighborhood and determine an escape route. The predators then take their time to ensure they have selected a suitable target, determine how to gain entry and what security measures can be observed from outside the residence.

Home invasion robberies can occur at any time when homes are likely to be occupied. Invaders rarely work alone and rely on overwhelming force and physical confrontation to gain initial control. The violence usually occurs during the initial 60 seconds of the confrontation, and home invaders frequently have handcuffs, rope, duct tape and firearms to subdue their victims and solicit their cooperation.

How to Avoid Being a Victim

First and foremost, you must always be aware of your surroundings and notice unusual activity. Avoid driving expensive and exclusive vehicles to commercial areas and be particular where you park. Underground parking garages can increase the danger if not patrolled by security since it affords predators various opportunities to hide inside the structure. When leaving a shopping area or any other venue and starting home, take the time to check your rear view mirror to notice if someone appears to be following you. If you detect a suspicious vehicle, do not return to your residence, drive to the closest police or fire station. Attempt to get a description of the vehicle, occupants and the license plate number. Be particularly suspicious of occupied, unfamiliar vehicles that are parked on the street near your home. Predators frequently wait for you to pull into your driveway and garage. They can be at your car door with a gun before you have the opportunity to exit your vehicle.

Following the security architecture recommendations outlined earlier will further reduce the likelihood of being a victim of home invasion. Ensure that your home has a high-quality security system connected to a central monitoring station that will immediately notify the local police. Signage stating your home is alarmed should appear in the front as well as the rear of your dwelling. Digital CCTV camera coverage to conduct perimeter surveillance and provide a history of events will greatly assist in investigative efforts if an invasion occurs.

Enclosing your property with a wall or fence and with access-controlled gate entry will form a natural barrier to define the confines of your property. Motion-activated intrusion lighting is relatively inexpensive but a great deterrent for someone creeping up on your home after dark.

Always identify any person seeking entry prior to opening gates or doors. Install camera coverage at all access points to verify the individual and speak through an intercom system (preferably voice/video so as to allow for visual observation and audio communication) to determine their business. If you suspect foul play, this gives you the opportunity to gather household occupants and retreat to a safe room while you summon authorities.

Likewise, some may choose to purchase a firearm to have in the house in the event of an intruder. This is not usually recommended unless members of the household have been thoroughly trained with firearms and have extensive experience handling a weapon. If small children are present, this may be a further reason not to maintain firearms in the home.

If you do decide to purchase a firearm to keep in the residence, be sure that you frequently visit a firing range and work with an instructor. You must understand the rules of engagement and the legal consequences if you fire the weapon at an intruder inside your residence (varies substantially by state). Lastly, ask yourself if you can take a life without hesitation if the situation dictates. This is not about merely being a good shot at the range but rather the ability to be hyper alert, control your stress and breathing, and pull the trigger without hesitation once the target has been identified. Even well-trained law enforcement personnel have hesitated, resulting in them being disarmed and killed with their own weapon (this isn't TV or the big screen).

Deploying armed security on your estate may be the best alternative if they are sufficiently trained and experienced in this area. This will further deter intruders and help protect the family if there is an intrusion attempt, without the need for family members to personally arm themselves.

Communicate with your neighbors and know their habits and vehicles. There is power and deterrence when your neighbors are watching your back and you are looking out for them.

Extortion and Blackmail

As we live through the current financial crisis, we see more individuals becoming the victims of extortion and blackmail. This is perpetrated by individuals attempting to obtain "insurance policies" by gathering negative material against their employer, spouse, lover or other targeted individual. The person then threatens to reveal substantially true but nonetheless damaging information about a person to the public, a family member or associates unless a demand is met. This information is usually of an embarrassing and/or socially damaging nature. Since the information is substantially true, the act of revealing the information may not be criminal in its own right and amount to a crime being committed. However, if the victim does not cooperate and they are threatened with physical injury to themselves or someone they love, in addition to public exposure of the information destroying an individual's reputation, this is a crime.

In some cases, the victim is told that an illegal act he or she had previously committed will be exposed to the public if the victim fails to comply with the demand. The crime involves a threat for purposes of compelling a person to do an act against his or her will, or for purposes of taking the person's money or property. Although blackmail is generally synonymous with extortion, the difference is that extortion involves an underlying, independent criminal act, while blackmail does not. There are three basic types of extortion:

- Bribery

- Blackmail

- Kidnap for ransom

Bribery is defined as any means of giving or offering something of value to a person in a position of trust who in return violates his or her duty or the law in order to benefit others. Bribery is a widespread crime that most often goes unreported. A bribe does not always have to be money. It can also consist of property, position or action.

Blackmail is defined as an attempt to extort money from a person by threatening to expose some damaging fact about the person or the person's past. Payment or nonpayment of the money makes no difference, for the crime is in the attempt to collect, influence or receive any other service that would constitute payment.

Kidnap for ransom is the detaining or taking of another person beyond the aid of family, friends and the law for the purpose of acquiring a ransom for his or her return. This is the most serious form of extortion under our current legal system.

If you are the victim of extortion, you need to seek professional help. Today, with the ease of obtaining electronic data from the Internet, extortionate demands often progress as follows:

- Demand made

- Send uploaded photos or video for verification

- Set payment terms

- If terms not met, make information public or cause physical harm

To minimize the risk of extortion, certain precautions can be taken:

• Don't think that someone will keep a secret

• Be extremely cautious of who you choose to socialize with and where (you never know when you are being recorded)

• Understand a breach of confidentiality may jeopardize your future

• Be cautious on the pictures you allow to be taken

• Remember this happens from Main Street to Wall Street and to the famous and non-famous alike

• Your actions will affect more than just you individually

• Share information or activities on a need-to-know basis

Chapter 12

KIDNAP & RANSOM

Adults, as well as children, have been kidnapped for centuries and for a variety of reasons. Today, most traditional kidnappings of the affluent are motivated by extortion or retaliation. Worldwide, most kidnap victims survive the experience. The victim is usually released after the ransom payment, though some victims have been severely injured or killed to prevent subsequent identification.

It is difficult to ascertain the accurate number of kidnappings that occur each year in the U.S. According to the U.S. Department of Justice, the number of kidnappings for ransom ranges between 600 and 700 annually. However, these are the kidnappings that are reported to law enforcement. There is an increasing presence of abductions that occur in the affluent community that are never reported to the authorities. One thing that is consistent is that kidnappings for ransom are not random acts. Much time is spent by the kidnappers prior to the actual abduction to determine the best time and location to make the abduction, providing them the greatest degree of success.

Affluent individuals are viewed by terrorist organizations and criminals as an easier means of obtaining significant money than committing other crimes. Kidnappings and extortions involving affluent individuals, corporate executives and their families are happening with alarming frequency. One of the most common crime scenarios involves the off-premises abduction of an affluent individual's employee and the subsequent demand for cash from the employer without involving law enforcement.

There is currently no law requiring kidnap cases to be reported to the authorities. There is also no law prohibiting families or firms from negotiating with the kidnappers and paying ransoms. In the U.S., kidnap cases are typically short-term events that last from only several hours to several days. U.S. kidnappings are oftentimes more likely to turn violent, since the kidnappers are often small-time criminals out to get a big payday. Once it becomes known that law enforcement is in hot pursuit, the abductors panic and cause harm to the hostage.

In other parts of the world, there are actually professional kidnappers trained as terrorists who approach the abduction as any other business dealing. They are predominantly carried out by groups that have the infrastructure and organizational capacity to track their targeted victims to discover the best time and place to stage the abduction and to hold them indefinitely while demanding a high ransom. They are prepared to wait out the victim's family and conduct negotiations over a period of months rather than days. They realize the hostage is their bargaining chip and they take precautions so no harm comes to him/her.

Whether the motivations of the kidnappers are due to economic or personal reasons, kidnappings have similar impact on the victim, his or her family, and business associates. For the victim, the experience is terrifying. Often confined in deplorable conditions, the detainee may be exposed to health hazards or subjected to threats or beatings that can lead to injury and even death. In the eventuality the victim is freed, it will have a profound psychological impact, which oftentimes results in paralyzing fear of being left alone. Throughout the detainment, the victim's family is also victimized being crippled by fear and uncertainty about the welfare of their loved one and not knowing if the situation will be resolved safely.

The threat of kidnapping is not something to be overlooked. However, the possibility of an abduction occurring can be significantly reduced since kidnapping is not a spontaneous event. Kidnappers must first learn of the individual's habits and vulnerabilities. This is conducted through surveillance, pretext phone calls and reviewing publicly available information. This is why it is imperative that affluent individuals embrace comprehensive security measures to avoid becoming a statistic.

In addition to the traditional kidnap for ransom, there are various other types of kidnappings for financial gain that have evolved over the years. The kidnapper, having become savvy to law enforcement involvement in past cases, appears to continually identify alternatives to redefine this moneymaking opportunity. Below are several trends currently in favor with the kidnapping criminal element:

- Express kidnappings

- ATM abductions

- Non-abduction extortion

Express Kidnappings

Express kidnappings remain a significant problem with victims held at gunpoint at an unknown location. There is no ransom demand or contact with the victim's family. The victim is robbed of their valuables and forced to provide their PINs and bank account information so their money can be withdrawn over a period of hours or days. This type of abduction is also popular for targeting individuals, such as financial managers, who have access to considerable sums of money through online accounts. Money will be transferred to the financial manager and the abductors will accompany him to the bank to make the withdrawal. Threats to family members are often made to ensure the individual's cooperation. Victims are usually found days later in seedy parts of the city, with no identification, commonly in a drug-induced stupor.

ATM Abductions

Victims are again held at gunpoint and driven to neighborhood ATMs to withdraw as much money as possible over a short period of time. These individuals are usually abandoned within hours in some remote location and have little information to provide police regarding their abductors.

Non-Abduction Extortion

Another trend that is emerging plays on an individual's fear of kidnapping. In this situation, criminals will observe their "victim" away from home and then call the family, claim (falsely) to have kidnapped the family member and demand an immediate ransom payment. The fact that this scam often proves successful demonstrates the extent to which our society lives in fear of kidnapping and ransom of loved ones.

From The RCS Files – A Walk in the Park
The subjects had identified their target, who they determined had the ability to raise $100,000 in cash on short notice. They knew the nanny went to the park each morning with the 5-year old daughter of her employer. Once at the park, the subject surreptitiously stole the nanny's phone and proceeded to call the victim's mother. The subject stated he had abducted her daughter and nanny, provided their clothing description and warned not to contact authorities or he would kill them both. She was then instructed to obtain $100,000 in the next 15 minutes and follow the stated delivery directions. The mother immediately tried to call the nanny, and the call was answered by the subject, stating she now had only 14 minutes to get the money or never see her daughter again. The money was obtained and the drop made, which was allegedly picked up by the subject's co-conspirator.

Once the nanny returned home with the child, she was unaware of why the police had been summoned or any understanding of the events that had just transpired. The subjects were never identified and the money never recovered.

Beginning of a Kidnapping or Extortion

Most kidnap/extortion situations are initiated with a telephone call from the perpetrator stating their demands. In the case of a kidnapping, the caller states emphatically that unless a ransom is paid, the victim will be killed or seriously harmed. In the case of extortion, a serious or deadly occurrence will take place if a specific demand is not met. Usually this call is made to the victim's immediate family, a friend, a business colleague or to the company where the victim is employed. Also the caller most likely will state not to contact law enforcement or the victim will be harmed or killed.

It is important that the person receiving this first call remains as calm as possible and does their best to obtain as much information as possible from the caller. If possible, training should be given to family members and employees regarding how to deal with these callers. It is very unlikely that the caller will stay on the telephone long enough to obtain any information other than the demand. If there is an opportunity to ask questions, be prepared to ask the following:

- Proof of life (an assurance that the victim is alive): ask to speak to the victim and obtain a description of victim's clothes, jewelry, etc.

- Take notes of what the caller says exactly and record the conversation if possible

- Listen for background noises such as airplanes, trains, church bells, etc.

- Try to get the caller to commit to a second call at a set time

- Reinforce your commitment to cooperate

• Establish a code name for the caller (this is necessary to avoid hoax callers in the event the kidnapping is later made public before the victim is released)

Surviving a Hostage Situation

The most dramatic and dangerous phase of any hostage situation is the moment of abduction. Without exception, resistance at this time is extremely dangerous, and the abductors may end up harming you when they had no intention to do so. You most likely will experience near paralyzing fear, so this is the time to cooperate as you begin to assess the situation. Your opportunity to escape may come and you can't afford to be injured, which would hamper your ability to take advantage of an opportunity when the time is right.

Your mental mindset is going to make the difference of surviving the experience intact or not. The following is a breakdown of former hostages' psychological reactions when held hostage for an extensive period of time:

Survivors	Nonsurvivors
Had faith	Felt abandoned
Contained hostility and aggression	Acted out
Maintained positive attitude	Self pity
Fantasized	Dwelled on present
Rationalized situation	Despaired
Kept to routines	Suspended
Controlled outward emotion	Acted out of control
Sought flexibility and humor	Withdrawn
Blended with peers	Stood out

Kidnap victims are oftentimes powerful individuals used to being in control of their environments. To survive this situation, they must understand the need to play a subordinate role to their abductors. When dealing with kidnappers, the victim must realize that they are no longer in a role of authority. The face of subservience must be presented to lull your captors into a belief of compliance. Remember that proper planning and preparation will result in survival.

Successful Coping Strategies

During the Abduction

• Normally the most dangerous phase of a hostage situation is at the beginning and, if there is a rescue attempt, at the end

• At the outset, the kidnappers are typically tense, high-strung and may behave irrationally so it is extremely important that you remain calm and alert and manage your own behavior

• Avoid resistance and sudden or threatening movements

• Do not struggle or try to escape unless you are certain of success

• Prepare yourself mentally and physically for a long ordeal

• Be confident people are working toward your release

Control Your Emotions

• Keep a mature, stable and controlled appearance

• Convey a sense of confidence

• Try to remain inconspicuous and avoid direct eye contact and the appearance of observing your captors' actions

• Consciously put yourself in a mode of passive cooperation

• Talk normally

- Do not complain, avoid belligerency and comply with all orders and instructions

- If questioned, keep your answers short and don't volunteer information or make unnecessary overtures

- Follow your routines vigorously and demonstrate a strong sense of self-preservation to your captors

- If you are involved in a lengthier, drawn-out situation, try to establish a rapport with your captors, avoiding political or religious discussions, or other confrontational issues

- Eat what they give you, even if it does not look or taste appetizing

Rationalize the Abduction

- No matter what the circumstances, never blame yourself for the abduction

- You must force yourself to rationalize and accept your actions

- You must focus on the fact that you are alive and a hostage and not use 20/20 hindsight

- You are clearly better off as a live hostage than a dead martyr

- Accentuate the positive

- Make the best of a difficult situation

Keep to Routines

- Establish a daily program of mental and physical activity to the extent allowed, which will greatly relieve stress

• Physical exercise provides a multitude of benefits

• Setting goals is an important way to mark progress; however, make sure they are realistic goals

• Don't be afraid to ask for anything that you need or want, such as medicines, books, pencils, papers, etc.

Strive to be Flexible and Keep a Strong Sense of Humor

• A flexible personality that will allow you to laugh at yourself and find humor in little things is crucial

• Even assigning the captors secret humorous names will relieve stress

• Maintain your sense of personal dignity and gradually increase your request for personal comforts; make these requests in a reasonable, low-key manner

Fantasize to Fill Empty Hours

• Many former hostages talk of their ability to escape mentally from their trauma by engaging in fantasy

• All agree that occupying empty hours—dealing with boredom—is one of the major problems of the experience

Blend With Your Peers (in the event of multiple hostages)

• Your chances of survival improve when you blend with your fellow captives

• Don't try to be a hero, endangering yourself and others

• The person who stands out—by being overly polite, crying or doing more than his or her share—brings unwanted attention to themselves and become an easy mark to exploit

• Do what you're told, but do it slowly

• Doing more than your captors demand is not a good survival technique

• Do not volunteer for assignments

Training to Survive

• Determine now, while you are calm and unstressed, what kind of person you are and how you will deal with a hostage situation Create a game plan in your mind that you will follow

• Visualize each element of an invented situation with a positive outcome

• Remember it is not what the abductors do to you and your fellow hostages but rather how you react to what they do to you and others

Things to Remember

• While every hostage situation is different, your chance of becoming a hostage is remote

• The U.S. government's policy is to not determine if a ransom payment should be made

• Your family can determine to pay a ransom

• Remember that you are a valuable commodity to your captors and it is important to them to keep you alive and well

• It is a federal felony to take a U.S. citizen hostage anywhere outside of the U.S.; therefore, the government will also be working on your safe return

Parental Abductions

From The RCS Files – The Vindictive Spouse
Weeks after having sold her privately held corporation for a substantial profit, an affluent female was served with divorce papers and advised that her husband would be seeking custody of their children. Shortly thereafter, she began to notice strange vehicles outside her home and consistently following behind her wherever she went. Not wanting this situation to come to the attention of the court and become even more public, she contacted RCS.

After meeting with the victim and assessing the threats, RCS deployed various stalking countermeasures such as TSCM, cyber audit, physical security, counter-surveillance and close personal protection. It was ascertained, through the intelligence garnered during this process, that the victim's husband had launched a complex harassment campaign with the intent of emotionally crippling the victim to the point she would agree to a quick divorce settlement and allow the husband custody of the children.

Methods deployed included placing a key logger on her laptop computer, removing money from joint bank accounts, installing covert microphones and video equipment in her home and vehicle, and maintaining close 24-hour surveillance on her to cause further intimidation. RCS was able to build a case against the husband and obtain law enforcement involvement that led to his and several others' arrests, which allowed the victim to retain custody of her children.

In the U.S., there has been an exorbitant increase in parental kidnappings over the past several decades. This is a direct result of the fact that divorce has become a common occurrence both in the U.S. and around the world. According to divorce statistics, it is estimated that 40–50 percent of first marriages end in divorce in the U.S. Second and third marriages have even higher divorce rates.

Parental kidnaps are situations where one spouse absconds with the child (oftentimes to other countries) while the other parent has legal or shared custody. These types of abductions can involve multiple jurisdictions and are frequently tied up in legal proceedings for extensive periods of time. Since there is not a ransom demand and there is no reason to believe the child is in jeopardy, law enforcement does not tend to allocate the extent of resources commonly used during traditional kidnapping for ransom investigations. Since each situation is inherently different you need to consult with a professional for guidance if confronted with this situation.

Chapter
13

STALKING AND
INAPPROPRIATE ACTS

From The RCS Files – A Woman Scorned

A prominent individual received a written death threat at his residence. Concerned that a police report might lead to public awareness/scrutiny, he immediately contacted his legal counsel, who in turn contacted RCS. A behavioral analysis of the letter was conducted, and a psychological profile of the author was determined. That information was conveyed to the client, who agreed to meet with an RCS consultant to discuss a confidential mitigation strategy.

The profile concluded the author was a female in her mid-20s displaying love-obsessed behavior and who felt she was being ignored by the victim. Her letter was intended to illustrate her displeasure with this treatment and the fact she would rather see him dead than with his wife. The letter also made it clear that the author had intimate knowledge of the lifestyle patterns of the victim's family.

Through conversation, it was learned that a substantial payment had previously been made to the author after she threatened to expose a previous relationship between them. The death threat was received when she was told that he would not be further victimized by providing continued payments for her silence.

Through interviews and investigation, it was ascertained that the author of the letter was friends with the nanny. She had introduced the subject to the client after revealing detailed, personal family information. The author was quickly identified, and she immediately discontinued all communication with the client and his family. The media was never apprised of the situation, physical security at the residence was reconfigured to emphasize anti-stalking procedures, the backgrounds of the household staff were re-evaluated and the threats ceased.

Nationwide, it is estimated that 5 percent of men and women will be victims of stalking at some point in their lives. At any given time, it is estimated that 200,000 women are being stalked in the U.S., while men make up a smaller but equally victimized group. The legal definition of stalking is defined primarily by state statutes. While statutes vary, most define stalking as a course of conduct that places a person in fear for their safety. Unwanted contact between a stalker and their victim, which directly or indirectly communicates a threat or places the victim in fear, can generally be referred to as stalking.

Crimes which may constitute stalking include threatening or harassing phone calls, vandalism, terrorist threats, peeping, trespassing, violation of restraining orders, arson and cyber monitoring. If you find yourself the object of excessive admiration or the recipient of inappropriate comments and other unwanted attention, you are possibly the victim of a stalker. You never want to underestimate the tenacity and resolve of a stalker. You may receive incessant phone calls, faxes, emails, flowers, gifts and possibly discover a new website has been constructed featuring you. This will accompany the numerous letters and notes left at your office or on your vehicle. You may begin to notice an increase in "chance" meetings with your pursuer. At the onset of these activities, you must take appropriate action to ensure your safety and understand the options available to you to resolve this situation.

Proactive Measures

• Stop all contact with your pursuer—there must be absolutely none. You may have the opportunity to give your pursuer one explicit rejection and after that no further contact. The pursuer does not want to be ignored. They will try to get you to agree to "one last meeting or conversation." If you agree, you have just encouraged their continued pursuit.

• Ensure you have an understanding of basic safety procedures and ensure these precautions are implemented into everyday life. However, they should be more strictly adhered to while you are a stalking victim.

• Contact the police if you are the victim of a criminal act or the stalker is a danger to you or others. Law enforcement agencies are limited in what they can do in situations where a violation of law has not occurred. Merely writing letters or calling a "friend" is not a violation of law. It is not universally recommended to contact the police in every instance. You want the police to have sufficient probable cause to arrest the stalker as opposed to simply warning the pursuer.

• Obtain a restraining order on a case-by-case basis. Historically, the earlier a temporary restraining order (TRO) is obtained after an explicit rejection, the higher the chances of success. On the other hand, getting a TRO after the victim has been actively pursued for a long period of time isn't likely to have the desired effect.

• Contact an experienced investigative firm that has investigated numerous cases of this type and brought them to successful resolution. There is no universal formula for success or a cookie-cutter approach to end a stalker's activities. Each case has to be evaluated individually and then a course of action identified to ensure the safety and end the unwanted pursuit of the victim. You need a firm with the knowledge and expertise to give you the guidance and provide the necessary intervention to successfully resolve the situation.

Threatening Communications

Imagine you are the victim of threatening or harassing phone calls and you need to figure out who is doing it and why. If you seek out a professional in this area, they will attempt to illicit the necessary information to make an accurate evaluation. However, that information is coming from you. You need to ask yourself not who made these threats, which most likely can't be answered, but rather who could have made these threats. With this approach, motives can be explored and, more than likely, a suspect will be identified.

We also have seen an increase in electronic extortionate threats. For example, extortion can include the threat of disseminating or divulging personal information, photographs or contractual information that could greatly harm the victim of the threat. With the ability to stream video and outlets, such as social networking sites and YouTube, millions of individuals can receive information with the click of a mouse. Those who have been victimized could have avoided this situation with some of the sample recommendations listed below:

- Setting up firewalls to protect access to systems

- Nondisclosure agreements with employees and third parties

- Password protection/encryption

- Controlled access to the Internet through servers rather than individual modems

Theft

Betrayal of trust is commonly the cause when affluent individuals are victims of theft and other crimes. Often the individual responsible is known by the family and frequently a trusted individual. These individuals feel they are entitled to something, rationalizing their indiscretions by believing they have "earned" the items through unfair treatment or that the items won't be missed. The devastating consequence to the victim is not so much the items stolen but the level of trust that was given to the individual responsible for the crime.

One of the fastest-growing opportunities for criminals not only in the United States but also in foreign countries is the market for stolen art. It is estimated that more than 100,000 pieces of art are stolen each year. Insurance companies pay between $3 billion and $5 billion per year on stolen art insurance claims. Most art thieves have access to private homes and steal art in order to sell it for fast money. Collectors and connoisseurs rarely perpetrate these crimes but end up purchasing the art for their collection without questioning if the seller had legal possession of the artwork. Art theft victims often recover their art in the hands of a subsequent, innocent buyer. When this happens, the courts are presented with a challenging dilemma.

Art theft differs significantly from the theft of other property. Valuable works of art can be relatively small, easily hidden and easily moved from the residence. Many thefts of art are never reported to the police, as victims are fearful that, if the theft is publicized, other thieves will identify them as a target and try to capitalize on their lack of security. Many also believe that media publicity regarding the theft will just drive the stolen item further underground.

From The RCS Files – Everyone is Suspect
A prominent celebrity residing in Nevada discovered she was the victim of a substantial jewelry theft. Concerned that a police report might lead to increased public exposure, she immediately contacted her legal advisor, who in turn contacted Risk Control Strategies (RCS). An investigation was initiated, and all signs quickly led to the belief that the thief was someone who was a trusted individual with complete access

to the celebrity's home. This information was conveyed to the client, who was in complete denial that it could possibly be a staff member since she trusted them explicitly and they were all long-term employees. She thoroughly believed it was someone from the construction crew that was remodeling her guest house. Earlier investigation had eliminated these individuals as potential suspects.

The client did not want us to interview any staff member unless we could first convince her why that individual should be considered a suspect. After conducting additional investigation, substantial information was developed convincing the client that the housekeeper, who had been employed by the family for over five years, was the primary suspect.

After interviewing the housekeeper, she eventually confessed to the crime, putting considerable blame on her new boyfriend who was pressuring her to steal. Eventually some of the jewelry was recovered from a pawn shop. The items were valued at over $350,000 and had been pawned for approximately five cents on the dollar. The employee was fired and the client did not wish to press criminal charges and face public exposure.

CHAPTER
14

THE THREAT OF TERRORISM

The threat of terror facing individuals from the U.S. is entirely different from years past. The intent is no longer focused on "publicizing
causes" but on the desire to destroy western civilization. This is being
fueled by the hatred for Christians and Jews; revenge for our presence
on Islamic soil; and religious extremists that define their success by the
number of American deaths they cause, the level of fear they can instill
and the amount of financial impact they have on our economy. Al-Qaida
is just one of several Islamic terrorist groups that have waged its jihad
against American interests. Intelligence reports, provided by the FBI
and Interpol, indicate al-Qaida continues to prepare for simultaneous
attacks in multiple countries, specifically targeting U.S. interests.

The likelihood of future airplane hijackings by terrorists is remote.
It is unlikely that passengers will quietly comply with hijackers
demands, based on what occurred on 9/11/01 and as recent as on

Christmas day 2009. However, the possibility of a terrorist attack at a major airport or even on board an aircraft cannot be overlooked. Our airport security needs improvement and needs to become more proactive rather than reacting to the latest security breech. Security strategies need to be developed that are truly effective in providing comprehensive security coverage for the air traveler from the moment they arrive at the airport until they are wheels up, en-route to their destination. Needless to say, for those who have the luxury of traveling on private aircraft, it is certainly the preferred mode of travel but not without its own specific vulnerabilities given the disparity in security between private and commercial airports.

Some examples of the reactionary security measures we have seen implemented are:

• A terrorist's attempt to light his shoes on fire during flight now requires passengers to remove their shoes at security

• A passenger was assaulted with a small pocket knife and, as a result, not even nail clippers were allowed to pass through security

• Airport security screens for metal objects while the explosives being used are made of plastic

• Several individuals tried to bring aboard liquid explosives; now travelers are restricted to no more than 3 ounces of liquids at security

• Warm food, now only served in first class, is accompanied by a metal fork and spoon but a plastic knife

• Efforts to bring down a flight arriving in Detroit on Christmas day with 278 passengers and 11 crew members aboard by a suspect with explosives sewn in his underwear launched an impulsive response from TSA limiting passenger movement, activities and the ability to use restrooms one hour prior to landing

Travelers have all experienced these continued fluctuations of new and inconvenient airport security measures when traveling. However, even though new threats impacting our security need to serve as wake-up calls, we cannot continue to merely react to the latest concern. Attacks, similar to what we see on the nightly news, further justify even more stringent and sustainable security solutions for the future.

There is a need to develop a comprehensive focus on security from the moment passengers enter the airport and not rely primarily on the TSA security checkpoint prior to entering the concourse. It would be extremely easy for someone to take a travel bag full of explosives and walk inside a busy airport and feign to temporarily leave the bag. Then it is simply a matter of walking outside and remotely detonating the explosives before security has time to react to the abandoned bag. We need to adopt policies, as in other countries, where security checks bags prior to entering inside the airport.

Since 9/11, there have been over 45 attacks overseas against Western-owned luxury hotels catering to U.S. travelers. Hotels located in Africa, Europe, South America, Middle East and Asia all had strict security measures in place. In spite of these enhanced security measures, there were no procedures to screen employees, who were later determined to be responsible for allowing explosives and suicide bombers to enter the various locations. Terrorists will continually be motivated to identify new techniques that will result in a high number of causalities and attract comprehensive media coverage to promote their cause.

As today's world continues to become a scarier place, terrorism will constitute an additional stage in the escalation of fear throughout the country. The threat of bombings and shootings at populated locations on U.S. soil is a reality. Over the past several years, numerous attacks, already in the planning stages, have been uncovered due to the outstanding work by law enforcement and intelligence agencies. Due to the classified nature of the operations, some of these you have read about, and others you haven't. Examples of well-publicized events include the Los Angeles International Airport and the New York City transportation system, both of which have been targeted on several occasions. Fortunately, these terrorist plots were discovered prior to being initiated.

Most likely, the next wave of attacks on U.S. soil will involve suicide bombers and improvised explosive devices (IEDs). These attacks will be characterized by simultaneous detonations against "soft targets" around the country, involving multiple cities and rural areas. Places where large groups of people congregate, such as stadiums, amusement parks, hotels, shopping malls, subways and casinos, will be sought-after targets. This, of course, does not leave out the potential of a NBCR (nuclear, biological, chemical or radiological) related attack which would cause devastating results to both human and financial assets.

Terrorists who want to destroy America prefer to use suicide bombers as a front-line approach. A suicide attack is the ultimate inexpensive and reliably lethal "smart bomb." Statistically, it is responsible for killing four times as many individuals than with other terrorist techniques, and there is an infinite abundance of young militants who are more than willing to receive their rewards promised in the life beyond. In a recent al-Qaida video, the chief spokesman declared, "Those youths that destroyed Americans with their planes did a good deed, and there are thousands more young followers who look forward to death as much as Americans look forward to living." However, not all future attacks will require suicide bombers. In many of the larger cities, terrorists can simply valet park a car loaded with explosives and walk away.

The backgrounds of the next level of terrorists, about which America should be most concerned, will not be coming from abroad. Instead these individuals will be "homegrown." They will have been educated in our schools and universities and work in metropolitan areas, and some will even serve in our military. These individuals will frequently travel back and forth to the Middle East for additional training. These young terrorists are most dangerous since they know our language and culture and will have a good concept of our habits as Americans; however, we will know little about them.

Future attempts to attack our homeland are imminent. Therefore, vigilance cannot be understated, and it has to become the responsibility of every individual in this country. Recent security evaluations were conducted and reported to Congress that involved placing an unattended briefcase in well-traveled locations in a variety of major cities. The results? Not one person called 911 or sought out law enforcement personnel to further investigate. In fact, in one city, someone actually attempted to steal the briefcase.

By comparison, in other nations where there is active terrorist activity, citizens are well-trained to immediately identify and warn publicly if a bag or package is unattended in a populated area. The area would then be quickly and calmly evacuated prior to law enforcement arrival. Fortunately, America hasn't yet had to experience the ongoing ravages of terrorism. Unfortunately, we are ill-equipped to fully understand the terrorist mindset, and we need to educate our citizens, who are inevitably the best first-line of defense against terrorism, for the security concerns we face.

So, what can America do to protect itself? First and foremost, we must embrace the fact that we are in the embryonic stages of a Holy War with a faceless enemy which will require we redefine certain freedoms so as not to compromise the future of our country. From an intelligence perspective, the U.S. needs to follow other nation's examples of developing hands-on human intelligence to augment satellite and electronic technology when evaluating terrorist activity. We need to converse with neighbors, co-workers and fellow students so we have the capability to identify suspicious or illegal activity and report to the appropriate authorities. We need to continue infiltrating targeted groups and solicit cooperation from trusted citizens to help. Lastly we need to engage and educate ourselves as citizens. We cannot afford to accept the role of being a mere observer of the war on terror; rather, we need to be active participants to ensure our own safety and that of our families. If we don't embrace this attitude, it will result in being a deadly mistake.

Every individual today must take on the personal responsibility to protect themselves and others against terrorist threats. Specifically, suspicious individuals, activity and packages need to be immediately reported to authorities. To accomplish this goal, it is important that we educate ourselves regarding the following:

- Who are suicide terrorists and how do they dress

- Women and children cannot be overlooked as potential suicide bombers

• Understand the tactics, mindset, targets and type of weapons

• Anticipate the consequences of an attack and develop a plan

• Assess your individual vulnerability; poor defenses make suicide terrorism possible

• Improve basic security measures in your daily life through awareness and prevention

• Understand pre-detonation and post-detonation considerations so you are not victimized as a first responder at a terrorism incident

Extremist Groups

Al-Qaida and other well-financed organizations are not the only threats of terrorism we face in the U.S. Eco-terrorists associated with animal rights, HIV research, oil spills, global warming and other movements are aggressively targeting corporate executives and employees. Safeguarding affluent individuals, their families and company assets, targeted by these radical extremist groups, is becoming increasingly more challenging. Their focus is strategic and unrelenting, which is directed towards delivering financial hardships as well as physical injury to these individuals and/or their loved ones. To validate this growing threat, these radical groups have been categorized by the FBI as the predominate domestic terrorism threat within our borders.

A thorough threat analysis of any high-profile individuals or firms that have become a target of these radical activists must be an ongoing process. Analysis of each event that impacts the company, its executives and employees must be conducted. As threats to global interests rise, it is increasingly important to have a security consultant with extensive risk management experience who can be relied upon to assist in developing planning, response and recovery protocols from those risks associated with doing business in today's challenging environment.

CHAPTER 15

CRAFTING THE GAME PLAN

As you can see, much must be done in order to properly care for the security needs of an affluent family. Hopefully, you have a renewed sense of appreciation for the time, thought, energy and effort that must be invested to formulate and implement all the necessary internal controls. However, what remains at the forefront for each advisor or family leader is what should be the next step. That said, drawing upon the information contained herein, we invite you to craft for your family, your practice or for each of your clients a strategic plan illustrating required next steps. So, grab a pen and fill in the sections below:

Goals

List every specific goal you wish to achieve in the following areas:

- Residential security

- Communications security

- Cyber security

- Staff/contractor due diligence

- Family office security

- Travel security

- Child-related security

- Personal security

- Business-related security

- Financial security and legacy protection

Obstacles

List all the foreseeable obstacles that could prevent the aforementioned goals from being achieved.

Strategies

List the corresponding strategies you will implement to overcome the defined obstacles.

Measurement

Formulate an evaluative instrument that will allow you to measure success.

We leave you with this strategic outline listed above. Let the conclusion of this book be the beginning of a new journey where you utilize the information you gleaned regarding family safety, legacy protection and personal security to achieve overall peace of mind. We hope you will consider this a reference guide to be referred to often when situations arise that you may have little familiarity with so you can validate you are doing the right things.

As you return to your active lives of emails, voice mails, meetings and travel schedules, begin to decide how you will implement the "best practice" procedures set forth herein. We ask you to keep in mind one last thought: What is your margin for error as it relates to the well-being of your family or the families you serve? This is not the time you should be willing to roll the dice and bet that everyone and everything is as safe and secure as possible merely because you believe it is so. Be certain because peace of mind is truly priceless, especially to those who know what it's like to have lost it.

APPENDIX A

Smart Home Network Architecture Questionnaire

The following checklist should be used to measure best practice compliance.

1. Have you ever conducted an audit or assessment of your information security posture? If yes, please indicate how long ago.
❑ Yes   ❑ No   ❑ Unsure
When:
Details:

2. Do you have any services, such as email, a website or other such Internet-based services, hosted at an off-site location? If so, please briefly describe them and how they are maintained.
❑ Yes   ❑ No   ❑ Unsure
Details:

3. Do you have password requirements? What is the minimum password length you specify? How often are they changed?
❑ Yes ❑ No
Minimum length/complexity required:
Changed every:

4. What antivirus software do you use on your servers and workstations? How often do you update it?
Details:

5. Do you regularly check for spyware/malware on your computers? If so, how?
❑ Yes ❑ No
Details:

6. Do you use any spam-filtering or other anti-spam measures, such as mail preprocessing? If so, please give brief details.
❑ Yes ❑ No
Details:

7. What type of firewall or other network security devices do you have protecting your connection to the Internet?
❑ Yes, connected ❑ No, not connected
Details:

8. Do you have any type of patch management solution implemented? If so, please describe it briefly.
❑ Yes ❑ No ❑ Unsure
Details:

9. Do you have any type of intrusion detection or prevention appliances analyzing your network?
❏ Yes ❏ No ❏ Unsure
Details:

10. Do you backup mission-critical data? How do you back it up? Is media stored locally or off-site? How often do you back it up?
❏ Yes ❏ No ❏ Unsure
❏ Tape ❏ CD/DVD ❏ Vaulting ❏ Other
❏ Local ❏ Off-site ❏ Unsure
Frequency of backups:

11. Do you compartmentalize and classify your data (i.e., sensitive, confidential, etc.)?
❏ Yes ❏ No ❏ Unsure
Details:

12. Do you have any data leak prevention methods deployed within your network?
❏ Yes ❏ No ❏ Unsure
Details:

13. How do you dispose of sensitive information?
Printed materials:
Electronic:

14. Do you have trained staff to provide computer support?
❏ Yes ❏ No

15. If you outsource your support, do you have a contract to maintain and/or fix your computers?
❏ Yes ❏ No ❏ Unsure

16. If you answered yes to questions 14 or 15, have you performed background investigations on your system administrators? Are they updated at least yearly?
❏ Yes   ❏ No   ❏ Unsure
Details:

17. Do you use encryption protocols on any of your network-attached devices, i.e., servers, workstations or portable devices?
❏ Yes   ❏ No   ❏ Unsure
Details:

18. Do you use portable electronic devices such as a PDA, Blackberry or smart phone? If so, are these devices password-protected and en-crypted?
❏ Yes   ❏ No   ❏ Unsure
Details:

19. Do you currently access your network remotely? If so, how is that connection accomplished? If known, describe the level of security pro-vided with your connection method.
❏ Yes   ❏ No   ❏ Unsure
Details:

20. Do you have a business continuity and/or disaster recovery plan in place? If so, when is the last time you tested your procedures?
❏ Yes   ❏ No   ❏ Unsure
Details:

Confidential Personal Profile

Name _____

      (Last)   (First)   (Middle)

Primary Residence _____

_____

Telephone (   ) _____

Secondary Residence _____

_____

Telephone (   ) _____

Occupation _____

Employer _____

Address _____

_____

Telephone (   ) _____

Physical Description and Background Information: _____

_____

_____

Date of Birth _____

D.L. # _____

Place of Birth _____

Height / Weight _____

Hair / Eyes _____

Scars / Marks _____

Physician _____

Address/Telephone _____

_____

_____

Medical Problems _____

_____

_____

_____

Blood Type _____

Dentist _____

Address/Telephone _____

_____

_____

Attorney _____

Address/Telephone _____

_____

Additional Comments _____

_____

_____

Spouse _____

Maiden Name _____

Date of Birth _____

D.L. # _____

Place of Birth _____

Height / Weight _____

Hair / Eyes _____

Scars / Marks _____

Physician _____

Address/Telephone _____

Medical Problems _____

_____

_____

_____

Blood Type _____

Occupation _____

Employer _____

Address _____

Telephone (   ) _____

Additional Comments _____

_____

Children - 1st _____
Date of Birth _____
Place of Birth _____
Height / Weight _____
Hair / Eyes _____
School _____
Residence Address _____
_____
Telephone (   ) _____
Employer _____
Address _____
_____
Telephone (   ) _____

Children - 2nd _____
Date of Birth _____
Place of Birth _____
Height / Weight _____
Hair / Eyes _____
School _____
Residence Address _____
_____
Telephone (   ) _____
Employer _____
Address _____
_____
Telephone (   ) _____

Children - 3rd _____
Date of Birth _____
Place of Birth _____
Height / Weight _____
Hair / Eyes _____
School _____
Residence Address _____
_____
Telephone (   ) _____
Employer _____

Address _____

_____

Telephone ( ) _____

Vehicles/Boats/Aircraft/Motorcycles _____

Vehicle 1 - Make _____

Year / Model / Color _____

License / State _____

Primary Driver _____

Vehicle 2 - Make_____

Year / Model / Color _____

License / State _____

Primary Driver _____

Vehicle 2 - Make_____

Year / Model / Color _____

License / State _____

Primary Driver _____

Relative/Close Associates/Domestic Employees _____

1. Name _____

Address _____

_____

Telephone ( ) _____

Relationship _____

2. Name _____

Address _____

_____

Telephone ( ) _____

Relationship _____

3. Name _____

Address _____

_____

Telephone ( ) _____

Relationship _____

Exec / Date_____

Spouse / Date_____

Child/Date _____

Child/Date _____

Child/Date _____

Additional Information _____

_____

_____

_____

Regularly Scheduled Activity _____

_____

_____

_____

_____

_____

_____

_____

_____

Miscellaneous (information to include residential deliveries, residential maintenance, frequent visitors, etc.) _____

_____

_____

_____

_____

_____

_____

_____

_____

_____

Obtain current photographs, fingerprints and DNA for all family members.

Readers
Reference
Guide

Crafting a Valid Threat Level

The following lifestyle categories must be examined carefully and specific descriptive responses to each component derived in order to craft the specific threat level:

• Travel Patterns – Mode, method, frequency, purpose and locations (domestic /international)

• Residences – Locations, security measures in place, event frequency, degree of valuables on site

• Yacht/Aircraft Ownership – Crew validation, locations maintained, frequency/purpose of use, chartered/leased agreements

• Philanthropic Activity – Events sponsored, how well publicized, frequency of contributions, public information available

• Business Interests – Type, industry, public or private, media coverage

- Religious Activities – Public information, level of involvement, previous concerns, collateral issues

- Political Involvement – Active campaigner, monetary support, frequency

- Personal Habits – Travel, collector, hobbies, events frequently attended, predictability of actions, tastes

- Social Involvement – Social functions, frequency, events hosted, media coverage

- Internet Usage – Family members, home office, financial trading, web surfing, gaming participation, banking

- Family Office Involvement – SFO/MFO internal controls, structure, personal participation, check signers

- Investment Strategy – Financial advisors, documented procedures and expectations, communication requirements

- Employee/contractor/advisor due diligence

Crafting the Family Security Plan

The following preparation and services should be incorporated into the construction of the family security plan:

- Background investigation and vendor/contractor screening program

- Due diligence investigations on current and future business associations/partnerships

- Investment intelligence (knowing with whom you are doing business)

• Security system planning and design

• Travel security and foreign travel advisory service

• Executive protection, both domestic and international

• Special events planning

• Identity theft protection, mitigation and response

• Crisis preparation and response

• Threat management

Crafting the Yacht Security Plan

The following measures should be considered during the preparation of the yacht security plan:

• Identify and confirm the background of crew

• Ensure confidentiality and NDAs are in place

• Conduct periodic TSCM (sweeps) on yacht to ensure privacy

• If weapons are on board, ensure appropriate training and storage

• Determine if vessel comes under new MTSA and IMO regulations (requirements for vessel security officer); if yes, ensure training requirements are met

• Obtain continual and advanced travel itinerary for client and determine risk for each intended location via a written threat assessment (travel to foreign ports should utilize firms with OSAC/DOS contacts)

• Evaluate terrorist potential, pirate activity, K&R risk, civil unrest, labor strife, etc., for areas of travel

• Ensure GPS tracking system has been installed on vessel so its location can be actively monitored

• Evaluate communication and IT security

• Establish emergency evacuation procedures

• Ensure appropriate medical equipment is on board and crew are trained to use

• Conduct physical security surveys for marina(s) and conduct risk assessment(s) to include policies and procedures, MTSA compliance, backgrounds of marina staff, etc.

• Evaluate overall threat to principal and his/her party and the impact on areas of travel

• Evaluate requirement for security personnel

Crafting the Aircraft Security Plan

The following measures should be considered during the preparation of the aircraft security plan:

• Identify and confirm the background of all pilots, flight crew and mechanics working on aircraft

• Determine if operating under FAR Part 91 or Part 135 and adhering to recommended TSA security requirements

• Validate all pilot licenses are current and review for FAA sanctions

• Validate they are in possession of a current medical card

• Ensure confidentiality and NDAs are in place

• Conduct periodic TSCM (sweeps) on aircraft to ensure privacy

• Develop a comprehensive written security plan

• Obtain continual and advanced travel itinerary for client and determine risk for each intended location of travel

• Conduct physical security surveys of fixed base of operation (FBO) where aircraft is maintained or areas frequently visited

• Ensure baggage remains in your possession and have a member of flight crew supervise baggage loading

• Identify and screen individuals responsible for the following:
    + aircraft cleaning (interior and exterior)
    + aircraft catering
    + aircraft refueling

• Ideally secure aircraft in enclosed hanger with interior security and surveillance system controlled and monitor by owner

Criteria when selecting an FBO

• Is the airport a controlled or uncontrolled airfield?

• What are the field operating hours?

• What is access control policy?

• What security procedures are in place to secure the facility?

• Is security staff on site at all times?

• Who has access to aircraft and vehicles?

- What was airport staff turnover percentage in the last year?

- Does perimeter fencing meet TSA security guidelines?

- Is the property patrolled?

- Is there adequate night lighting?

- Are crash/fire/rescue vehicles stationed on site?

- What is the fire department's response time?

- Are FAA-compliant background checks performed annually on all personnel with routine access to airport facilities or aircraft?

- Are fingerprints and photos submitted with all background checks?

- Is drug testing regularly performed on all personnel?

- Are all persons with tarmac or aircraft access required to wear photo ID?

- Are security cameras available and in proper working order?

- Are hangars controlled by aircraft owner or FBO?

- Is there fuel farm/truck security?

- Is emergency power available?

- How are aircraft secured?

- How many vehicles are authorized for on-airport use?
- Are unknown vehicles screened and escorted?

- Are drivers screened and licensed?

• Are all vehicles entering parking areas screened?

• Are all parking areas monitored via security cameras?

Physical Security Architecture Checklist

Whether building a home or purchasing an existing one, the security system strategy that should be followed is as follows:

• Obtain current site plan

• Conduct thorough background investigations on all contractor personnel to avoid having known criminals and illegal aliens work on your home

• Assess outer perimeter risks (water, woods, public roads and/or unfettered adjoining property access); it's wise to know who your neighbors are

• Design the outer and inner perimeters of the property
+ Larger properties – driveway entrance/access gate, etc.
+ Inner perimeter – pool/tennis court access

• Research average local law enforcement response times

• Consider an intrusion system to include an underground perimeter sensing cable that provides warning that an intruder has trespassed onto your property long before they reach your front door

• Assess CCTV location for complete coverage to eliminate blackout zones or potential for compromise

• Incorporate appropriate illumination (remember, if you cannot obtain facial recognition, you are wasting your money)

• Ensure proper exterior and interior wiring is installed to include CAT 5, CAT 6 and alarm device cables

• Due to unique specifications and potential difficulty in installation, outdoor cabling requirements must be thoroughly considered prior to construction

• Assess the method of utility wiring from the street poles to your home and consider underground conduit installation to better protect and secure electrical and telephone service

• Evaluate safe room locations, design and potential costs

• Assess lighting requirements (aesthetically pleasing yet productive)

• Have ability to light up premises inside and out with the flick of a switch

• Ensure all exterior doors and windows are alarmed properly

• Ensure inclusion of glass break and motion detection technology and all life safety/environmental devices

• Ensure installation of wireless and hardwired silent panic buttons

• Ensure alarm panel can integrate entire system for easy use

• Ensure that the security alarm system has backup batteries to provide power in the event of a home power loss. It should be noted that it is not uncommon for the more educated intruder to disable power prior to entering the home

• Ensure placement of interior and exterior alarm sounders
    + Interior sounders should be installed in areas of your home where you may not be able to hear the alarm
    + Exterior sounders will alert your neighbors and guide the first responders directly to your front door

• Most high-end security system keypads have silent ambush and panic alarm features; ensure these features are programmed and activated and that you are properly trained in their use

• Ensure that proper backup communications to the alarm panel is in place; cellular backup will provide communications to the alarm central station in the event that the alarm panel phone lines are cut or tampered with

• Ensure that daily test signals are sent to the central station from the main security alarm panel and the cellular back up alarm panel; these tests should be logged by central station personnel and acted upon in the event a test signal is not received

• Ensure that members of the household and work staff each use a unique ID code to arm and disarm the alarm panel (alarm ID codes should be changed annually) so as to establish and maintain access accountability

• Ensure that the security system is connected to a secure home network with full encryption installed to guard against hacking

• Thoroughly screen the intended alarm/video monitoring company (central station monitoring company contracts must be closely scrutinized)

Safe Room Construction

The following requirements should be taken into consideration for any safe room construction:

• Construction spans floor to ceiling

• Steel stud walls faced with steel sheet and/or bullet-resistant materials such as Kevlar

• Masonry construction may be possible alternative

• Bullet-resistant door with internal steel framing

- Single control point to firmly secure door

- Flame retardant wall material

- Sound-proofing to muffle noise

- Finish with sheetrock or other decorative finish consistent with the room

- Ceilings constructed similar to walls

- Floors capable of carrying excessive load

- Ensure fresh air intake and exhaust

- Ductwork passing through protected walls needs to protect from poisonous gasses being inserted into the safe room

- Video monitor to access camera system and be sure to locate camera outside safe room

- Alarm system access

- Multiple communication systems

Additional Accessory Considerations

- Toilet capability

- Flashlights with extra batteries

- Fresh water

- Non-perishable foods

- First aid items

• Gas masks

• Required medication

• Specialized medical equipment

Communication Security Protocols

Best practices call for the following measures:

• Do not leave your computer unattended when you are logged on.

• If you are not using it, turn off internet connection.

• Do not leave your password unsecured anywhere - especially close to your computer

• Change passwords frequently

• Control access to your computers and backups

• Be sure to log off when done with the computer

• Maintain an appropriate level of protection for all laptop computers by remembering the following:
> + Provide appropriate protection and security at your residence
> + Never leave a laptop in plain view inside a vehicle
> + Never leave a laptop unattended anywhere, for any length of time. This includes airports, train and bus stations, vehicles, meeting rooms, hotels, etc.
> + Never check in a laptop computer as luggage
> + Ensure all critical information is backed up and maintained in a secure location

• Install a dedicated server within the home to act as the communication brain (for the affluent client, this calls for a step above the typical firewall solution, which house standard algorithms that more experienced hackers can bypass easily)

• Integrate all house phones (preferably VOIP), cell phones, security systems and Internet connection through secure servers

• Monitor system with comprehensive event logging

Child Protection Protocols

The following red flags should be avoided at all costs when selecting staff that will have access to children:

• Referrals from friends or acquaintances (apologies don't suffice post-incident)

• Internet/newspaper advertisements (this is not where you find the right people)

• Employment/placement agencies who you take at face value that they are thoroughly vetting prospects

• Foreign-born individuals without written proof of legal alien status (look up USC Title 8, § 1324 and ask yourself if going to jail for five years is an option you want to consider)

• Self-initiated backgrounds (if childcare is not what this person does for a living, don't experiment with your children)

Oftentimes, we can make some minor lifestyle modifications to increase security and safety for our children. The following security precautions can be easily implemented:

• Lose the vanity plates (no reason to drive you and your children around in a vehicle that can be easily recognized or remembered)

• Be aware of any strangers loitering on street corners or around the neighborhood

• Note vehicles that are often parked up the street but still in line of sight of the house

• Take down suspicious license plate numbers and description of the vehicle and occupants

• Note vehicles that seem to cruise the neighborhood

• Do not open the door to anyone unless the person is positively identified

• Do not tell strangers, shopkeepers or tradesmen about family travel plans

• Families should avoid consistent travel patterns when working, shopping or attending social activities

• When planning a trip, do not stop services and deliveries but rather let friends or staff members handle these matters during your absence

• Do not jog or walk near the home at the same time each day. Make certain that outside doors are secured and alarm set when both at home and away from residence

• Never leave young children at home unattended. Instruct caregivers to keep the doors and windows locked and to never let in strangers

• Teach the children as early as possible how to call the police should strangers or prowlers loiter around the house or attempt to gain entry

• Keep the house well lit when you are at home

• Avoid obvious indications that your home is unattended or absent adults (e.g., garage doors left open with no vehicles inside)

• Limit or monitor participation in social networking sites

• Refrain from electronically sending personal pictures

• Monitor any Internet gaming

• Educate children on the messages they send via email, text or instant messages, as they are often misused

• Consider installing a family-based server within the home that provides enhanced security for desktop and laptop computers

• Install disc-level encryption and GPS tracking on all the laptop computers

• Limit Internet purchases to known sites and use a separate credit card with a low limit for these transactions only

• Consider biometric or facial recognition software to control unauthorized access to laptops

Background Investigation Checklist

The following is a sampling of the minimum background information that should be examined when conducting backgrounds on individuals:

• Character, reputation and integrity of individual

• Criminal and civil litigation history in local, state and federal courts

• Education verification

• Prior job history verification

• Verification of licenses required for employment

- Address history

- Credit history

- Bankruptcy/liens/judgments

- Sexual predator list

- Watch list (global criminal)

A sampling of the background information that should be examined as a minimum in each venue when conducting backgrounds on businesses is as follows:

- Extensive research on the firm and its principals

- Prior bankruptcies

- Liens/judgments

- Corporation filings

- Proper licensing

- Business filings in state(s) doing business

- UCC filings

- Associated businesses and principals

- Internet domain names registered to business

- Current and previous property ownership

- Current motor vehicles registered to individual

- Dun & Bradstreet report

- Better Business Bureau

The following interview techniques can assist in conducting a successful interview:

- Thoroughly prepare for the interview
    + Methodical review of application
    + Consider communication barriers such as language, culture, gender, emotions, etc.

- Establish control, rapport and credibility with individual

- Do not ask too many questions initially

- Convince individual to be straightforward

- Do not allow theme of questioning to shift

- Determine if direct or indirect questions are best based upon the personality of individual

- Ask leading questions, which contain answers or a choice of answers

- Be continually alert for inconsistencies in answers

- Practice active listening

- Do not interrupt or finish other person's sentence

- Continually monitor nonverbal communication
    + Eye contact
    + Body movement
    + Voice pitch
    + Facial expressions
    + Gestures

• At termination of the interview ask, "Is there anything else I did not ask or anything you want to add?"

Family Office Protection Protocols

Operational Security

• Are security policies and procedures in place, such as access control, visitor escorting, document security and communications security?

• Are HR policies compliant and enforced to avoid employment law issues?

• Is a security training and operational awareness program in place for both office and house staff?

• Are thorough background investigations conducted on employees and contractors prior to hiring for the office and the families' homes?

• Are disaster recovery (DR) plans documented and DR exercises conducted on a yearly basis to test systems for failsafe preparedness?

• Are nondisclosure/integrity assurance agreements in place for all employees and contractors?

• In protecting family information from theft and extortion, are technical surveillance countermeasure (TSCM) inspections periodically conducted?

• Is investigative due diligence conducted for family members prior to committing monies to investments or donations?

• Is the family name protected from unneeded exposure on the Internet?

• Are crisis preparedness and response plans in place to protect the family in the event of exposure to such issues as kidnap for ransom, extortion, stalking, child abduction, home invasion, hate crimes and terrorist attacks?

Physical Security

• Are access controls in place for all external ingress/egress points?

• Should bulletproof glass been installed in the principal's office?

• Are strategically installed CCTV cameras installed in all critical areas?

• Are all critical IT systems integrated within an encrypted server and appropriately protected through the use of locked area, software and hardware devices?

• Has glass-break technology been strategically installed within the offices where appropriate?

• Are all exterior electrical and communications cabinets locked and monitored for breach?

• Are fire control detection systems in a secured area?

• Is confidential trash properly disposed of to ensure destruction?

• Are controlled access procedures in place for cleaning crews, contractors and maintenance personnel, or are they permitted unfettered access to the office when no one is there?

• Are families' homes professionally secured in relation to the exposure their wealth creates (see chapter on Securing the Home Front)?

Systems Security

• Is a qualified patch management process in place for all workstations and servers?

• What type of user identification, authentication and authorization process controls are in place throughout the environment?

• Are application security controls in place?

• Are wireless network access points necessary? If they are, are they appropriately protected with the latest authentication mechanisms?

• Are sensitive data exchanges secured and are data classification levels on critical databases enforced?

• Are data or email encryption technologies in place to protect sensitive information leaving your server and desktop environments?

• Are intrusion prevention controls in place across the network?

• Are the NAC (network access control) hardware and policies valid and reliable?

• Is the firewall administration outsourced?

• Are there any types of intrusion detection system (IDS) or intrusion prevention systems (IPS) present?

• Are incident response procedures currently in place?

• Are procedures, to include appliance and device documentation, documented and secure, off-site storage?

• Are response methods (i.e., battery backup times, recovery timelines for critical systems, equipment and data backups, etc.) in sync with expectations of management?

• Are network administration capabilities controlled by only qualified network administrators?

• Are network administrators monitored for their activity? Does executive management maintain a separate administrative user name/password, or does the IT manager have the "keys to the kingdom?"

• Are regular, external IT security audits conducted to ensure level of security measures are appropriately in place and operational?

• Are IT protocols in place and exercised when employees are terminated (i.e., downloaded and archived email profiles, user access terminated, etc.)?

Personal Security

Are procedures in place, and have all appropriate family members (including children) provided security awareness information and seminars on the following topics?

• Stalking

• Identity theft

• Kidnap for ransom (to include express kidnap scenarios)

• Extortion

• Safe dating

• Travel awareness

• Child protection

• Self defense

• Adverse media containment

• Are travel itineraries protected and are travel agents thoroughly screened?

• Is investigative due diligence conducted prior to the acquisition of aircrafts and yachts and are TSCM inspections conducted prior to travel by new owners?

• Are personal protection protocols in place?

• Are risk assessments conducted on each venue prior to family members traveling and reports generated for family review?

• Are contingency plans in place to assist family members while traveling in the event an emergency evacuation is required?

• Are children/young adults traveling without an adult escort educated on the risks of abduction and general safety protocols?

Internal Financial Controls

Comprehensive security-related policies must be formulated and implemented on the following subject areas:

• Fund transfers

• Bookkeeping/reconciliation protocols

• Protection from unauthorized investment transactions

• Authorizations/limits/access – procedures that safeguard access to funds

• Improper allocation of investment funds

• Recording cash receipts

• Disbursements

• Payroll controls to eliminate fraud – ghost employees

• Segregation of duties – investments, financial accounting, reporting

Travel Security Protocols

Pre-Travel

• Limit travel itinerary to a "need to know" basis; delegate someone as a 24/7 contact and arrange daily communication protocol

• Every traveler should have a system of accountability for tracking family members while traveling; this information must be limited to involved parties only and never discussed outside that inner circle

• Provide prearranged car service, submitting segments of travel only

• Ensure no signs are presented to identify the individual traveling by name at the airport

• Identify alternative routes of travel, including different modes of transportation, to provide prompt response in the event of a crisis

• Select a separate credit card to be used for all travel reservations and accommodations

• Make copies of wallet contents and passport/visa prior to travel

• Ensure all required medication is packed in carry-on bags

• Remove all forms of identification from travel bags by substituting them with other identifying features

• There is no reason to advertise who you are or where you live; one alternative is to place a tag with your business address without company name on your bags; in the event you are claiming a lost bag, your picture ID with proof of business address will suffice

• Bring and utilize luggage ties to secure luggage and ensure the safety of your belongings while they are left unattended in a hotel room

• It is recommended to not register or make reservations in your own name if you are well known and prone to attracting unwanted attention

• When possible, book hotel rooms between the second and seventh floors to limit first floor access while still being positioned safely for emergency evacuation if necessary

• Obtain foreign currency in advance consisting of small denominations and avoid carrying large sums of cash

• Program cellular phones with local one-touch emergency telephone numbers

• Identify medical facilities in and around the area(s) of destination in advance

• Bring a copy of passport, driver's license and related visa documents to be kept in a separate location in the event of being lost or stolen

• Ensure daily communications are scheduled in advance with point of contact (POC)

• Develop consistent code words/phrases to alert POC to an adverse situation

While Traveling

• Always maintain a low profile

• Avoid routine patterns and vary travel routes

• Be conscious of being followed

• Never leave a laptop unattended and only travel with needed data by utilizing removable media/data storage

• Affix an identification label to the outside of laptop to avoid confusion of ownership while processing through secure checkpoints

• Morning arrivals and departures are recommended

• Take caution when conversing with strangers despite their personal appearance

• Avoid traveling with items that are not absolutely necessary

• Limit items to be carried

• Dine in recognized eateries not off the beaten path

• Avoid street vendor food

• While flying, remain at the entrance of the metal detector until your bags have gone through the X-ray machine and never let them out of your sight for any time period

• If flying commercially, once on the plane, keep your carry-on beneath your seat in lieu of in the overhead compartment

• While traveling by train, enter and remain in only those cars that are occupied

• Do not joke about weapons and/or explosives

Upon Arrival

• Keep door bar locked while in the room

• Avoid all public areas of the hotel as criminal/terrorist activity is drawn to these areas

• Do not, under any circumstances, discuss the nature of the trip with anyone and be cautious of the information discussed over the telephone

• Avoid nighttime activity away from the hotel if feasible

• If away from hotel, always watch drinks while they are being poured and never leave them unattended

• Be sure any time a credit card is used it is promptly returned, and do not give it to bartender to establish a tab

• Avoid using your own name when making social reservations

• Ensure that daily contact is made with the delegated point of contact (POC) and contingencies are developed

• Leave your passports in the hotel safe (providing it is a well-known, internationally recognized property)

• Carry a card with personal medical information, including blood type, medications (including those causing allergic reactions) and physician contact numbers, at all times

• Only use ATMs during the day and preferably inside a bank.

• Beware of pickpockets and the common techniques they use (distractions, such as jostling, spilling something on you, asking for directions, the time, solicitation of items, and small groups, oftentimes of children, that you must pass through)

Identity Theft Avoidance Measures

• All personal checks should display name and address other than personal residence

• All charitable donations should be made under the name of the company/fund in lieu of the family name to avoid unnecessary exposure

• All documents containing personal information such as social security number, date of birth, address, medical insurance information, credit card numbers and PINs should be shredded with confetti-cut or pulverizing shredders prior to discarding

• If personal information is stored electronically, ensure it is properly encrypted

• Avoid mail delivery to your personal residence

• Internet purchases should only be done with one specific credit card for this purpose only, and the card should have a very low credit limit

• Use unique passwords and PINs on all accounts avoiding mother's maiden name, spouse's name, anniversary/birth dates and children's names

• Examine your credit report once per quarter to ensure no unauthorized activity (more frequently if a problem is detected). Remember, when this is done by others, it registers as an inquiry and can adversely affect your beacon score

• Ensure that all doctor's offices utilized have implemented and enforce Health Insurance Portability and Accountability Act (HIPAA) procedures

• If utilizing a travel agency, ensure best-practice security measures are in place to protect all your personal information and travel itinerary

• Independently verify the legitimacy of all calls or correspondence prior to opening dialogue

• Do not verify any information someone already has about you

• Do not cash a check or transfer money for anyone who is a mere acquaintance

• Never provide SSN online or over the phone

• Never log into any of your online accounts from a link you received via email

• Do not believe anyone can get you a new SSN account number

• Place a fraud alert or extended fraud alert on your credit report

• Provide updated contact information to all credit bureaus

• Review credit reports from all reporting agencies annually

• If you suspect fraud notify organizations possibly affected, close accounts and change passwords and PINs

Kidnap Coping Strategies

During the Abduction

• Normally the most dangerous phase of a hostage situation is at the beginning and, if there is a rescue attempt, at the end

• At the outset, the kidnappers are typically tense, high-strung and may behave irrationally, so it is extremely important that you remain calm and alert and manage your own behavior

• Avoid resistance and sudden or threatening movements

- Do not struggle or try to escape unless you are certain of success

- Prepare yourself mentally and physically for a long ordeal

- Be confident people are working toward your release

Control Your Emotion

- Keep a mature, stable and controlled appearance

- Convey a sense of confidence

- Try to remain inconspicuous, and avoid direct eye contact and the appearance of observing your captors' actions

- Consciously put yourself in a mode of passive cooperation

- Talk normally

- Do not complain, avoid belligerency and comply with all orders and instructions

- If questioned, keep your answers short and do not volunteer information or make unnecessary overtures

- Follow your routines vigorously and demonstrate a strong sense of self-preservation to your captors

- If you are involved in a lengthier, drawn-out situation, try to establish a rapport with your captors, avoiding political or religious discussions, or other confrontational issues

- Eat what they give you, even if it does not look or taste appetizing

Rationalize the Abduction

• No matter what the circumstances, never blame yourself for the abduction

• You must force yourself to rationalize and accept your actions

• You must focus on the fact that you are alive and a hostage and not use 20/20 hindsight

• You are clearly better off as a live hostage than a dead martyr

• Accentuate the positive

• Make the best of a difficult situation

Keep to Routines

• Establish a daily program of mental and physical activity to the extent allowed, which will greatly relieve stress

• Physical exercise provides a multitude of benefits

• Setting goals is an important way to mark progress; however, make sure they are realistic goals

• Don't be afraid to ask for anything that you need or want: medicines, books, pencils, papers, etc.

Strive to be Flexible and Keep a Strong Sense of Humor

• A flexible personality that will allow you to laugh at yourself and find humor in little things is crucial

• Even assigning the captors secret humorous names will relieve stress

• Maintain your sense of personal dignity and gradually increase your request for personal comforts; make these requests in a reasonable, low-key manner

Fantasize to Fill Empty Hours

• Many former hostages talk of their ability to escape mentally from their trauma by engaging in fantasy

• All agree that occupying empty hours—dealing with boredom—is one of the major problems of the experience

Blend with Your Peers (in the event of multiple hostages)

• Your chances of survival improve when you blend with your fellow captives

• Do not try to be a hero, endangering yourself and others

• The person who stands out, by being overly polite, crying, or doing more than their share, brings unwanted attention to himself or herself and becomes an easy mark to exploit

• Do what you are told, but do it slowly

• Doing more than your captors demand is not a good survival technique

• Do not volunteer for assignments

Training to Survive

• Determine now, while you are calm and unstressed, what kind of person you are and how you will deal with a hostage situation

• Create a game plan in your mind that you will follow

• Visualize each element of an invented situation with a positive outcome

• Remember it is not what the abductors do to you and your fellow hostages but rather how you react to what they do to you and others

Things to Remember

• While every hostage situation is different, your chance of becoming a hostage is remote

• The U.S. government's policy is not to determine if a ransom payment should be made

• Your family can determine to pay a ransom

• Remember that you are a valuable commodity to your captors and it is important to them to keep you alive and well

• It is a federal felony to take a U.S. citizen hostage anywhere outside of the U.S.; therefore, the government will also be working on your safe return

Statistical

Information

KIDNAPPED &

MISSING INDIVIDUALS

National Crime Information Center (NCIC) (SOURCE)

• In 2008, there were 778,161 missing person reports logged on their system. Of those reported missing, 87,497 were listed as being in physical danger, and 20,562 were kidnapped.

+ As the United States is estimated to have a population of about 304 million people, if 20,562 persons were reported kidnapped in 2008, it would amount to a kidnapping rate of 6.7 per 100,000 persons.

• Of the 589,761 juveniles reported missing in 2008, 13,046 were considered to have been in physical danger. Of those, 6,094

were considered to be kidnapped.
> + During this period, the U.S. population was estimated at 74 million persons under age 18; resulting in a kidnapping rate among persons under 18 of 8.2 per 100,000.

• As of December 20, 2007, there were 105,229 active missing person records in NCIC. Juveniles under the age of 18 accounted for 54,648 (51.93%) of the records, and 12,362 (11.75%) were for juveniles between the ages of 18 and 20

• In 2007, there were 518 records entered as Abducted by a Stranger; 299,787 entered as Runaway; and 2,919 entered as Abducted by Non-Custodial Parent. This only accounts for 303,224 entries of the 418,967 entered, or 72.4%, which is an increase from 297,632 entries of the 836,131 entered, or 35.6%, in 2006

• Kidnapping for ransom is a common occurrence in various parts of the world today, and certain cities and countries are often described as the "Kidnapping Capital of the World." As of 2007, that title belongs to Baghdad. In 2004, it was Mexico, and in 2001 it was Colombia. Haiti also has frequent kidnappings (starting several years ago), as do certain parts of Africa

• Only a tiny fraction, around 10%, of all kidnapping cases are reported to authorities for fear that it will trigger further kidnappings

The United States Department of Justice (SOURCE)

• 797,500 children (younger than 18) were reported missing in a one-year period of time studied resulting in an average of 2,185 children being reported missing each day

• 203,900 children were the victims of family abductions

• 58,200 children were the victims of non-family abductions.
115 children were the victims of "stereotypical" kidnapping. "Stereotypical" kidnappings have the following characteristics:

+ The child victim does not know their abductor (or has only a slight acquaintance)

+ The child victim is held overnight, transported 50 miles or more

+ The child victim is either killed, a ransom demanded, or the abductor intends to keep the child permanently

+ 33% of the missing children are family or "friends of the family" abductions. The 2000 US census population for children is 71,623,390. Based upon these statistics, the chances of family or "friends of the family" abducting a child in any given year is about .36% (36 children abducted per 10,000)

Kidnap Outcomes

• Most kidnaps are carried out in order to obtain a ransom, and in most cases a ransom is paid

• Rescues are rare (most authorities in most countries consider the safety of the victim is paramount)

• The average occurrence of deaths following a kidnap is 9%

• The death of the victim usually occurs at the time of abduction, rather than during negotiations

Kidnap Demands & Payments

• Ransom demands can be huge, with more than 14 countries recording cases of $25 million or more in recent years

• Kidnappers usually settle at between 10 and 20 percent of the demand, with the exception of the Former Soviet Union, where the mafia is extremely reluctant to negotiate and uses excessive violence to achieve its aims

• While most ransom payments are kept confidential, recent years have seen a noticeable increase in the ransoms paid. While many Latin American countries and Iraq have had multiple kidnappings that resulted in high ransoms being paid, many of the largest settlements have been made in Europe. Recent years have seen a noticeable increase in average ransom payments

Oil, Petrochemical and Energy Risks Association (OPERA)
http://www.oilpera.co.uk/presentations/terrorism.pdf

• More than 30,000 kidnaps occur each year; 55% of worldwide kidnaps are in Latin America

• The number of kidnaps is increasing around the world

• Average ransom payments are on the increase

• Over 70% of kidnaps are resolved by ransom payment

• Less than 10% of victims are rescued

United Nations Survey on Crime Trends and the Operations of Criminal Justice Systems – 8th Report (2002 Statistics)

Kidnappings by Country (2002)

# 1	United Kingdom:	3,261 kidnappings
# 2	South Africa:	3,071 kidnappings
# 3	Canada:	2,933 kidnappings
# 4	Belgium:	994 kidnappings
# 5	Tunisia:	555 kidnappings
# 6	Peru:	491 kidnappings
# 7	Portugal:	432 kidnappings
# 8	Romania:	383 kidnappings
# 9	Kuwait:	281 kidnappings
# 10	New Zealand:	257 kidnappings

# 11	Japan:	205 kidnappings
# 12	Switzerland:	203 kidnappings
# 13	Italy:	124 kidnappings
# 14	Poland:	118 kidnappings
# 15	Saudi Arabia:	107 kidnappings
# 16	Germany:	88 kidnappings
# 17	Croatia:	80 kidnappings
# 18	Chile:	74 kidnappings
# 19	Bolivia:	46 kidnappings
# 20	Czech Republic:	28 kidnappings
# 21	Lithuania:	26 kidnappings
# 22	Luxembourg:	23 kidnappings
# 23	Azerbaijan:	20 kidnappings
# 24	El Salvador:	19 kidnappings
#25	Latvia:	16 kidnappings
#25	Denmark:	16 kidnappings
#25	Costa Rica:	16 kidnappings
#28	Albania:	15 kidnappings
#28	Hungary:	15 kidnappings
#30	Belarus:	14 kidnappings
# 31	Cyprus:	12 kidnappings
#32	Slovakia:	10 kidnappings
#33	Austria:	9 kidnappings
#34	Slovenia:	8 kidnappings
#34	Uruguay:	8 kidnappings
#36	Morocco:	6 kidnappings
#37	Oman:	5 kidnappings
#38	Finland:	2 kidnappings
#38	Iceland:	2 kidnappings

Total: 13,973 kidnappings

(SOURCE)
The Straits Times, March 17, 2007

Xinhua General News Service, February 5, 2007

Schinnerer& Co., 2002-2004.

World Kidnapping Statistics—Regional Breakdown

• 73% Latin America (Colombia, Mexico, Ecuador, Venezuela and Brazil)

• 15% Asia Pacific (India and the Philippines)

• 5% Europe

• 4% Africa (Nigeria, South Africa)

• 3% North America

World Kidnapping Statistics—Most Common Victims

• 27% Dependents

• 23% Business personnel

• 15% Other

• 14% Non-professional employees

• 8% Government officials and security forces

• 6% Professionals, including journalists

• 4% Ranchers

• 3% Project workers, including engineers

Home Invasion

The Federal Bureau of Investigation (FBI) Uniform Crime Statistics Report

- One property crime happens every 3 seconds

- One burglary occurs every 10 seconds

- One violent crime occurs every 20 seconds

- One aggravated assault occurs every 35 seconds

- One robbery occurs every 60 seconds

- One forcible rape occurs every 2 minutes

- There were over 2 million burglaries in 2005

- An increase in burglary offenses was the only property crime to increase in 2005 compared with the prior year data

United States Department of Justice

- 38% of assaults and 60% of rapes occur during home invasions

- 1 of every 5 homes will experience a break-in or home invasion (over 2,000,000 homes)

- According to Statistics Canada, there has been an average of 289,200 home invasions annually over the last 5 years

- Statistically, there are over 8,000 home invasions per day in North America

- 50% of home invasions involve the use of a weapon; the most common weapons used are knives or other cutting instruments

• In 48% of home invasions, victims sustain physical injuries

• Victims age 60 or older make up 17% of home invasion victims

• In 68% of home invasions, victims and the accused are strangers; in 11% of these cases, victims and the accused are friends, business associates, or family

Violent Crime

The Federal Bureau of Investigation (FBI)

2009 Uniform Crime Statistics Report (2008 Statistics)

• An estimated 1,382,012 violent crimes occurred nationwide, showing a decrease of 1.9% from the 2007 estimate. The 2008 estimated violent crime total was 1.6% above the 2004 level but 3.1% below the 1999 level

• There were an estimated 454.5 violent crimes per 100,000 inhabitants in 2008

• Aggravated assaults accounted for 60.4% of violent crimes, the highest number of   violent crimes reported to law enforcement. Robbery accounted for 32.0% of violent crimes, forcible rape - 6.4%, and murder - 1.2%

• In 2008, offenders used firearms in 66.9% of the nation's murders, 43.5% of robberies, and 21.4% of aggravated assaults

• An estimated 16,272 persons were murdered nationwide. This was a 3.9% decrease from 2007, a 0.8% increase from 2004, and a 4.8% increase from 1999

• There were an estimated 5.4 murders per 100,000 inhabitants, a 4.7% decrease from 2007

• 89.4% of the murders that occurred in the United States in 2008 were within Metropolitan Statistical Areas, 6.3% were in non-metropolitan counties, and the remainder (4.3%) occurred in cities outside metropolitan areas

• In 2008, the estimated number of forcible rapes (89,000 - the lowest figure in the last 20 years) decreased 1.6% from 2007, was 6.4% lower than 2004, and 0.5% below the 1999 level

• The rate of forcible rapes in 2008 was estimated at 57.7 offenses per 100,000 female inhabitants, a 2.4% decrease when compared with the 2007 statistic of 59.2

• Rapes by force comprised 92.5% of reported rape offenses, and attempts or assaults to commit rape accounted for 7.5% of reported rapes, according to data reported to the UCR Program in 2008

• In 2008, the estimated robbery total (441,855) decreased 0.7% from the 2007 estimate. However, the 5-year robbery trend (2004 data compared with 2008 data) showed an increase of 10.1%

• The estimated robbery rate (145.3 per 100,000 inhabitants) showed a decrease of 1.5% from 2007

• Losses estimated at $581 million were attributed to robberies, with the average dollar loss per robbery offense was $1,315. The highest average dollar loss was for banks, which lost $4,854 per offense

• Firearms were used in 43.5% of robberies in 2008. Strong-arm robberies accounted for 40.2% of the total

• In 2008, there were an estimated 834,885 aggravated assaults (274.6 offenses per 100,000 inhabitants) in the nation

• According to 2- and 10-year trend data, the estimated number of aggravated assaults in 2008 declined 2.5% and 8.4%, respectively, when compared with 2007 and 1999

• A comparison of 10-year trend data for 2008 and 1999 showed that the rate of aggravated assaults in 2008 dropped 17.9%

• Of the aggravated assault offenses for which law enforcement agencies provided expanded data in 2008, 33.5% were committed with blunt objects or other dangerous weapons; 26.2% involved personal weapons such as hands, fists and feet; 21.4% were committed with firearms; and 18.9% involved knives or other cutting instruments.

Property Crime

The Federal Bureau of Investigation (FBI)

2009 Uniform Crime Statistics Report (2008 Statistics)

• There were an estimated 9,767,915 property crime offenses in the nation in 2008

• The 2-year trend showed property crime decreased 0.8%, compared with 2007. The 5-year trend, comparing 2008 with 2004, showed a 5.3% drop in property crime

• The rate of property crimes was estimated at 3,212.5 offenses per 100,000 inhabitants, a 1.6% decrease when compared with 2007. The 2008 property crime rate was 8.6% lower than 2004, and 14.2% lower than 1999

• Larceny-theft accounted for 67.5% of all property crimes in 2008. Burglary accounted for 22.7% and motor vehicle theft for 9.8%

• An estimated 17.2 billion dollars in losses resulted from property crimes in 2008

• In 2008, there were an estimated 2,222,196 burglaries—an increase of 2% when compared with 2007 data

• There was an increase of 3.6% in the number of burglaries

compared with 2004, and an increase of 5.8% from 1999

• Burglary accounted for 22.7% of the estimated number of property crimes committed

• Of all burglaries, 61.2% involved forcible entry, 32.3% were unlawful entries (without force) and the remainder (6.4%) was forcible entry attempts

• Victims of burglary offenses suffered an estimated $4.6 billion in lost property in 2008; overall, the average dollar loss per offense was $2,079

• Burglaries of residential properties accounted for 70.3% of all burglary offenses

• There were an estimated 6.6 million (6,588,873) larceny-thefts nationwide or 2,167 per 100,000 inhabitants

• The rate of larceny-thefts declined 0.5% from 2007 to 2008, and the rate declined 15.0% from 1999 to 2008

• Larceny-thefts accounted for an estimated 67.5% of property crimes

• The average value of property taken during larceny-thefts was $925 per offense; the loss to victims nationally was nearly $6.1 billion

• Thefts of motor vehicle parts, accessories and contents made up the largest portion of reported larcenies—35.8%

• Nationally, 62,807 arson offenses were reported by 14,011 law enforcement agencies that provided 1-12 months of arson data. Of those agencies, 13,980 provided expanded offense data concerning 56,972 arsons

• Arsons involving structures (residential, storage, public, etc.) accounted for 43.4% of the total number of arson offenses; arsons involving mobile property accounted for 28.9%; and other types of property (such as crops, timber, fences, etc.) accounted for 27.7% of reported arsons

• The average dollar loss per arson offense was $16,015

• Arsons of industrial/manufacturing structures resulted in the highest average dollar losses (an average of $212,388 per offense)

•In 2008, arson offenses decreased 3.6% when compared with the 2007 number

• Nationwide, the rate of arson was 24.1 offenses for every 100,000 inhabitants

Identity Theft

Identity Theft Resource Center
http://www.idtheftcenter.org

• As many as 10 million Americans a year are victims of identity theft

• 38% - 48% of victims find out about the identity theft within 3 months of it starting

• 9% - 18% of victims take 4 years or longer to discover that they are victims of identity theft

• Victims spend from 3 to 5,840 hours repairing damage done by identity theft.

• 26% - 32% of victims spend a period of 4 to 6 months dealing with their case and 11% - 23% report dealing with their case for 7 months to a year

Monetary Costs of Identity Theft

• 40% of business costs for individual cases of identity theft exceed $15,000. The Aberdeen Group has estimated that $221 billion a year is lost by businesses worldwide due to identity theft

• Victims lose an average of $1,820 to $14,340 in wages dealing with their cases

• Victims spend an average of $851 to $1,378 in expenses related to their cases

Practical and Emotional Costs of Identity Theft

• 47% of victims have trouble getting credit or a loan as a result of identity theft

• 19% of victims have higher credit rates and 16% have higher insurance rates because of identity theft

• 11% of victims say identity theft has a negative impact on their abilities to get jobs

• 70% of victims have trouble getting rid of (or never get rid of) negative information in their records

• 40% of victims experience stress in their family lives as a result of displaced anger and frustration over the identity theft.

• 45% of victims feel denial or disbelief

• 85% of victims feel anger and rage

• 45% of victims feel defiled by the identity thief

• 42% of victims feel an inability to trust people because of the identity theft

• 60% of victims feel unprotected by the police

Uses of Victim Information

• 43% of victims believe they know the person who stole their identity

• 14% to 25% of victims believe the imposter is someone who is in a business that holds their personally identifying information

• The most common reported perpetrator in cases where a child's identity is stolen is the child's parent

• 16% of identity theft victims are also victims of domestic harassment/abuse by the same perpetrator. These victims believe that the identity theft is used as another way for the abuser to continue and demonstrate his harassment and control

• More than one third of victims report that identity thieves committed checking account fraud

• 66% of victims' personal information is used to open a new credit account in their name

• 28% of victims' personal information is used to purchase cell phone service

• 12% of victims end up having warrants issued in their name for financial crimes committed by the identity thief

Responsiveness to Victims

• Overall, police departments seem to be the most responsive to victims of identity theft, with 58% taking down a report on the victim's first request

• 1/3 of victims have to send dispute information repeatedly to credit reporting agencies

• Only 1/5 of victims find it easy to reach someone in a credit reporting agency after receiving their credit report.

• 20% of victims will have the misinformation and errors removed from their credit report after their first request for the credit reporting agency to do so.

Fraud

Consumer Fraud Reporting: Crime Statistics
http://www.consumerfraudreporting.org/internet_scam_statistics.htm (SOURCE)

AMOUNT LOST BY SELECTED FRAUD TYPE FOR INDIVIDUALS REPORTING MONETARY LOSS

Complaint Type	Percentage of Reported Total Loss	Of those who reported a loss, the average (median) $ Loss per Complaint
Check Fraud	7.8%	$3,000.00
Confidence Fraud	14.4%	$2,000.00
Nigerian Letter Fraud	5.2%	$1,650.00
Computer Fraud	3.8%	$1,000.00
Non-delivery (Merchandise & Payment)	28.6%	$800.00
Auction Fraud	16.3%	$610.00
Credit/Debit Card Fraud	4.7%	$223.00

• Non-delivered merchandise and/or payment were the most reported offense, accounting for 32.9% of referred complaints

• Internet auction fraud accounted for 25.5% of referred complaints

• Credit/debit card fraud made up 9.0% of referred complaints

• Confidence fraud ("con men"), computer fraud, check fraud, and Nigerian letter fraud (also called "Advance Fee Fraud" or AFF) round out the top seven categories of complaints referred to law enforcement during the year.

Identification of Perpetrators

• 77.4% Male

• 50% resided in one of the following states: California, New York, Florida, Texas, District of Columbia and Washington

• The majority of reported perpetrators (66.1%) were from the United States; however, a significant number of perpetrators where also located in the United Kingdom, Nigeria, Canada, China and South Africa

Identification of Victims:

• 55.4% Male

• Nearly half were between the ages of 30 and 50, and one-third resided in one of the four most populated states: California, Florida, Texas and New York

• While most were from the United States (92.4%), Immigration Customs Enforcement (ICE) received a number of complaints from Canada, United Kingdom, Australia, India and France

• Males lost more money than females (ratio of $1.69 dollars lost per male to every $1.00 dollar lost per female). This may be a function of both online purchasing differences by gender and the type of fraudulent schemes by which the individuals were victimized

• Email (74.0%) and web pages (28.9%) were the two primary mechanisms by which the fraudulent contact took place

• The greatest concentration (per capita) of Internet scammers in the United States is concentrated in the District of Columbia (Washington, D.C.) and Nevada. By sheer numbers, California, New York and Florida take the top three positions, based on their population sizes

• Globally, in 2008, most scammers operated from the United States. The U.S. still held a huge lead in active Internet users then, a gap that has since closed considerably

• In 2008, China and the U.S. each had approximately 200 million internet users, and most of the world has grown commensurately

• Several countries stand out in 2008 as have disproportionately huge populations of scammers: Nigeria, Romania, the Netherlands and China. Lottery and fake money transfer (AFF) frauds seem to be the specialty of the Nigerians

• The United States still leads in identity theft and phishing/spoofing frauds

Top Ten Countries by Count (Perpetrators)

1. United States — 66.1%
2. United Kingdom — 10.5%
3. Nigeria — 7.5%
4. Canada — 3.1%
5. China — 1.6%
6. South Africa — 0.7%
7. Ghana — 0.6%
8. Spain — 0.6%
9. Italy — 0.5%
10. Romania — 0.5%

• Perpetrators also have been identified as residing in the United Kingdom, Nigeria, Canada, Romania and Italy. Interstate and international boundaries are irrelevant to Internet criminals. Jurisdictional issues can enhance their criminal efforts by impeding investigations with multiple victims, multiple states/counties and varying dollar losses

Stalking

Stalking Resource Center

The National Center for Victims of Crime

Stalking Victimization

• 3.4 million people over the age of 18 are stalked each year in the United States

• 3 in 4 stalking victims are stalked by someone they know

• 30% of stalking victims are stalked by a current or former intimate partner

• Persons aged 18-24 years experience the highest rate of stalking

• 1 in 4 victims report being stalked through the use of some form of technology (such as email or instant messaging)

• 10% of victims report being monitored with global positioning systems (GPS), and 8% report being monitored through video or digital cameras, or listening devices

Impact of Stalking on Victims

• 46% of stalking victims fear not knowing what will happen next

• 29% of stalking victims fear the stalking will never stop

• 1 in 8 employed stalking victims lose time from work as a result of their victimization and more than half lose 5 days of work or more

• 1 in 7 stalking victims move as a result of their victimization

• The prevalence of anxiety, insomnia, social dysfunction and severe depression is much higher among stalking victims than the general population, especially in instances where the victim is being followed or had property destroyed by the stalker

Recon Study of Stalkers

• 2/3 of stalkers pursue their victims at least once per week, many daily, using more than one method

• 78% of stalkers use more than one means of approach

• Weapons are used to harm or threaten victims in 1 out of 5 cases

• Almost 1/3 of stalkers have stalked before

• Intimate partner stalkers frequently approach their targets, and their behaviors escalate quickly

Intimate Partner Femicide

• 76% of intimate partner femicide victims have been stalked by their intimate partner

• 67% had been physically abused by their intimate partner

• 89% of femicide victims who had been physically assaulted had also been stalked in the 12 months before their murder

• 79% of abused femicide victims reported being stalked during the same period that they were abused

• 54% of femicide victims reported stalking to police before they were killed by their stalkers

Stalking Laws

• Stalking is a crime in all 50 states, the District of Columbia, and the U.S. Territories

• Less than 1/3 of states classify stalking as a felony upon first offense

• More than 1/2 of states classify stalking as a felony upon second or subsequent offense or when the crime involves aggravating factors

• Aggravating factors may include: possession of a deadly weapon, violation of a court order or condition of probation/parole, victim under 16 years, or same victim as prior occasions

• During a 12-month period, an estimated 14 in every 1,000 persons age 18 or older were victims of stalking

• About half (46%) of stalking victims experienced at least one unwanted contact per week, and 11% of victims said they had been stalked for 5 years or more

• The risk of stalking victimization was highest for individuals who were divorced or separated—34 per 1,000 individuals

• Women were at greater risk than men for stalking victimization; however, women and men were equally likely to experience harassment

• Victims often don't report stalking to law enforcement; only 37% of Male and 41% of female stalking victims came forward, mostly out of fear of being taken seriously

• Approximately 1 in 4 stalking victims reported some form of cyber stalking such as email (83%) or instant messaging (35%).

SOURCES

National Crime Information Center

The United States Department of Justice

Oil, Petrochemical and Energy Risks Association (OPERA)
http://www.oilpera.co.uk/presentations/terrorism.pdf

"10 Countries You're Most Likely to Get Kidnapped In"
Written by: Dave Emery
(September 2008)

United Nations Office on Drugs and Crime, Centre for International Crime Prevention

UN Survey on Crime Trends and the Operations of Criminal Justice Systems (8th ed., 2002)

The Straits Times, March 17, 2007

Xinhua General News Service, February 5, 2007

Schinnerer & Co., 2002-2004

Federal Bureau of Investigation - 2009 Uniform Crime Report
http://www.fbi.gov

Identity Theft Resource Center
http://www.idtheftcenter.org

Consumer Fraud Reporting: Crime Statistics
http://www.consumerfraudreporting.org

Stalking Resource Center

The National Center for Victims of Crime

United States Department of Agriculture
Departmental Management
http://www.da.usda.gov/pdsd/Security%20Guide/Spystory/Industry.htm